The Amazing Collection

The Kingdom Books
Teaching Curriculum

Joshua Through 2 Kings

No part of *The Amazing Collection*, whether audio, video, or print may be reproduced in any form without written permission from Big Dream Ministries, Inc. P.O. Box 324, 12460 Crabapple Road, Suite 202, Alpharetta, Georgia 30004
1-678-366-3460
www.theamazingcollection.org

ISBN-13: 978-1-932199-59-8
ISBN-10: 1-932199-59-4

By Big Dream Ministries

Cover design by Melissa Swanson

Some of the anecdotal illustrations in this book are true to life and are included with the permission of the persons involved. All other illustrations are composites of real situations, and any resemblance to people living or dead is coincidental.

Unless otherwise identified, all Scripture quotations in this publication are taken from the *New American Standard Bible (NASB)*.
© The Lockman Foundation 1960, 1962, 1968, 1971, 1972, 1973, 1975, 1977, 1995

Printed in the United States

INTRODUCTION TO THE KINGDOM BOOKS
Set Two: Joshua through Second Kings

The Kingdom Books continue the story of Israel from Deuteronomy as Moses had now died and Joshua became the leader of the nation. Now the people were ready to enter the Promised Land. Under Joshua's capable leadership, the land was conquered and divided for the twelve tribes. For the next approximately 350 years, Israel was a theocracy, occasionally served by judges who led the people to break the yoke of oppressing nations.

The book of Ruth is a love story that illustrates the concept of the kinsman-redeemer. First Samuel introduces the first king, Saul, who fails to lead the people and leaves the nation in turmoil and defeat. In 2 Samuel, Israel's second king, David, succeeds in uniting the people and stabilizing the nation under God. First Kings tells of the golden years under Solomon, followed by the civil dispute that divided the nation into Israel and Judah. Second Kings continues the monarchy until Israel is destroyed by Assyria and Judah is conquered and exiled by Babylon. The Kingdom Books begin with a war of victory and end with a war of defeat and destruction. In between are stories of great spiritual victory and horrendous spiritual failure as Israel struggled to live in obedience to their God. These books cover approximately eight hundred years from 1405 to586 B.C.

As you begin The Kingdom Books, the participants will begin a new workbook. It would be helpful to take a few moments with new students to review the format of the class and the workbook. Pointing out the charts (especially the Chronological Relationship of the Old Testament Books on page 199), the maps on page 200–206, and the concept of the Complete Read and the Quick Read, will be a great help to them.

Remind them that the Kingdom Books continue history from the Pentateuch so it is important to take some time for a quick review of the events and the people in those first five books. The Pentateuch Review from the book of Deuteronomy in the Teaching Guide Set One will help you if you need a little refresher yourself!

Again encourage the students to do all of their homework and to keep in mind that they are learning for life so you will be reviewing and reviewing the main characters and events in each book on a weekly basis. And above all, enjoy the journey through this incredible book, God's Holy Word!

Those in exile would live in Babylon for seventy years and, as God had promised in the Book of Jeremiah, He would bring them back to the land He had promised Abraham.

THE TEACHING GUIDE BULLETS/BOXES

Below is a reference guide explaining the bullet points. Do not let these become a stumbling block — they were designed to make the teaching outline easier to follow. Please note that the material presented in the boxes for "Teaching Tip," "Note," and "Application" may be used as time allows or you feel appropriate for your particular class.

Remember: your main goal is to share God's story!

▪	**Teaching Outline Points**	These are the teaching notes that come directly from the lessons taught by Pat Harley, Eleanor Lewis, Margie Ruether, and Linda Sweeney. They follow the student workbook's outline.
~	**Additional Teaching Notes**	
⋆	**Further Detail**	These are additional teaching notes that bring greater detail to each lesson.
✹	**Teaching Tip**	The information contained in these boxes is designed to give you more information — whether on background or culture or context.
◆	**Note**	
❋	**Illustration**	These "stories" are designed to directly support the points being made in the lesson. If you would prefer to use personal illustrations and/or applications, please be very sure that your personal story directly supports the lesson being taught in the workbook. Don't, however, fall prey to simply sharing a good story! Text may also emphasize a point by presenting a thought-provoking question.
❖	**Application**	
✝	**Scripture References**	These are specific scriptures being cited. We have used the New American Standard Bible (NASB).
⇨	**Summary Points**	These summarize an important "take-away" from the section being taught.
⌗	**Reviewing What We've Learned and Final Thoughts**	Repetition is a great teaching tool. These bullet points reiterate important topics with the goal to help those in your Bible study to "remember to remember." They will be used within the lesson and at the end in "Final Thoughts."

JOSHUA

Land Conquered

So the LORD gave Israel all the land which He had
sworn to give to their fathers, and they
possessed it and lived in it.

Joshua 21:43

SESSION SIX: JOSHUA
Land Conquered

✞ **Memory Verse:** *"So the Lord gave Israel all the land which He had sworn to give to their fathers, and they possessed it and lived in it".* (Joshua 21:43)

- **Introduction:** The book of Joshua is a continuation of history that began with the book of Genesis. At the end of the Pentateuch, in the book of Deuteronomy, the children of God were poised once again on the shores of the Promised Land. They had just spent forty years wandering in the wilderness and the rebellious generation had all died as had Moses. Now Joshua was ready to lead the younger generation into the Promised Land.

- **Oral Review:** Please refer to the **REVIEW Section** in the following Teaching Guide Outline.

- **Homework:** Take this time to review the homework from the book of Deuteronomy if the students have brought their books to class. Some of the questions that should be discussed are:

  The two questions at the top of page 138
  The middle of page 143
  The middle of page 145–147
  The questions on page 149

- **Review Helps:** Written review is provided at the end of the teachers' presentation. (Optional and time permitting.)

- **Teacher Presentation on the Book of Joshua**

- **Learning for Life Discussion questions:** You may choose to discuss all or just one or two of the questions on page 31.

- **Closing prayer:** Pray that the students would grow in their faith in the Lord so they might have the courage and strength of Joshua in order to face any battle that would come their way.

JOSHUA
Theme: Land Conquered

TIMELINE AID FOR TEACHERS:

- **Joshua 1**   God commissioned Joshua to be the leader of the Israelites
- **Joshua 2**   The spies canvassed Jericho
- **Joshua 3**   God parted the Jordan River and the people crossed
- **Joshua 4**   They settled at Gilgal
- **Joshua 5**   The men were circumcised
                   The people celebrated Passover
                   Manna stopped
- **Joshua 6**   They conquered Jericho
- **Joshua 7**   They were defeated at Ai
                   They cleansed the sin from the camp and Achan was killed
- **Joshua 8**   They defeated Ai
- **Joshua 9**   The Gibeonites deceived the Israelites
- **Joshua 10**   The southern coalition was defeated (southern cities)
- **Joshua 11**   Northern Canaan was defeated
- **Joshua 13-19** Land was divided
- **Joshua 20**   Cities of refuge were established
- **Joshua 23**   Joshua's farewell message was given
- **Joshua 24**   Three burials

JOSHUA
[Land Conquered]

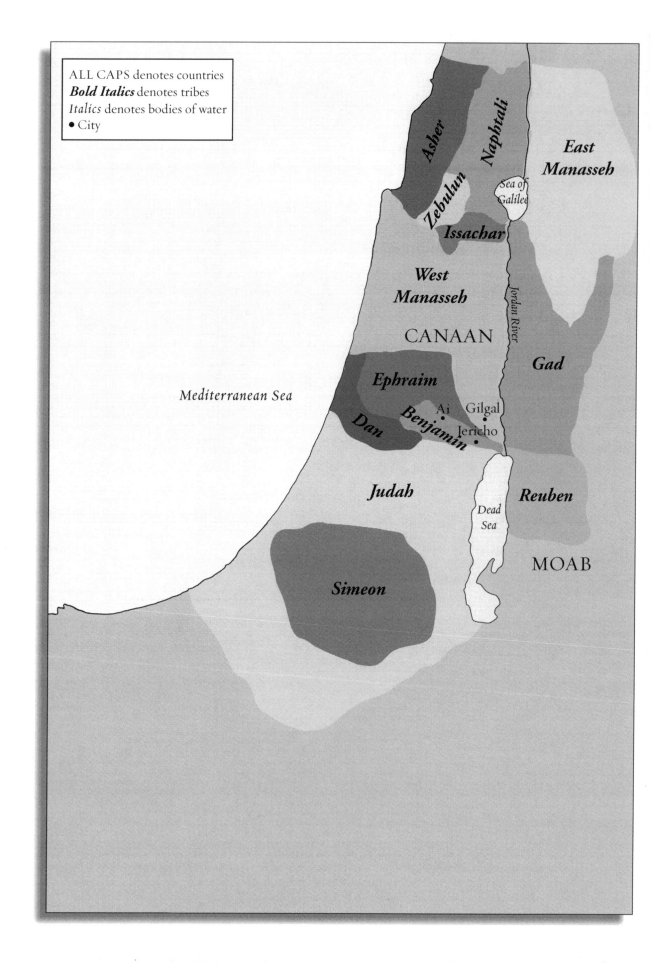

ALL CAPS denotes countries
Bold Italics denotes tribes
Italics denotes bodies of water
• City

Asher

Naphtali

East Manasseh

Zebulun

Sea of Galilee

Issachar

West Manasseh

CANAAN

Jordan River

Gad

Ephraim

Ai •

Gilgal

Benjamin

Dan

Jericho •

Reuben

Mediterranean Sea

Judah

Dead Sea

MOAB

Simeon

JOSHUA
Theme: Land Conquered

THE BASICS:

⇨ **Who: The Author:** Joshua
    Main Character: Joshua
⇨ **What:** Conquering and settling the Promised Land
⇨ **When:** The book covers 25 years (1405–1380 B.C.)
⇨ **Where:** Almost entire book takes place in Canaan
⇨ **Why:** The Israelites, led by Joshua, conquered and settled the land God promised them

MEMORY VERSE: *"So the Lord gave Israel all the land which He had sworn to give to their fathers, and they possessed it and lived in it." Joshua 21:43*

****

REVIEW:

GENESIS

⌗ The book of beginnings.
  1. The beginning of the human race.
     * The beginning of sin and its consequences, death and separation from God.
  2. The beginning of the chosen race.
     * The beginning of a promised solution—a Savior Who would be a descendant from Abraham's family.
⌗ Abraham's family would become a great nation and be given land.

EXODUS

⌗ The book of deliverance.
⌗ God grew Abraham's family of seventy into a great nation while they were in bondage in Egypt.
⌗ God powerfully and miraculously delivered the Israelites from that bondage and took them to Mt. Sinai where He prepared them for living by giving laws for society, morality, and religion.
⌗ God gave the people plans for building a tabernacle for Him where He would dwell in their midst.

LEVITICUS

⌗ The book of holiness.
⌗ God gave further instructions for holy worship and holy living.
⌗ The people were to be holy, which means "set apart for God and His service." This would make them different from those living around them.

JOSHUA
Theme: Land Conquered

NUMBERS
- ☐ The book of unbelief.
- ☐ The people came right to the edge of the Promised Land, but in unbelief they rebelled and refused to enter the land.
- ☐ Because of fear, they saw the people living in the land as giants, and themselves and God as grasshoppers.
- ☐ This unbelief and disobedience had a consequence. Instead of entering the Promised Land they wandered for forty years in the wilderness until this entire generation had died.

DEUTERONOMY
- ☐ The book of obedience.
- ☐ The people learned that God is a God of second chances.
- ☐ God repeated His laws to the new generation and prepared them to enter the land of promise.
- ☐ He encouraged them to teach their children about the works of God and the Word of God.
- ☐ God promised blessings for obedience and curses for disobedience.

OVERVIEW:
- Over 500 years had passed since God promised Abraham that He would give his descendants a special land.
- God chose Moses to bring the people out of Egypt and lead them into that Promised Land.
- Moses faithfully guided, trained, interceded, and sacrificed for the people. He died before the people entered the land.
- Joshua replaced Moses as the Israelite's leader.
- The Israelites that Joshua led were obedient and devoted to God, ready to move forward in faith and face the mighty Canaanites with courage.
- The book of Joshua covers twenty-five years of Israel's history.
  - ~ The first seven years were of battle and the conquest of Canaan.
  - ~ It took eighteen years for the land to be divided and settled. (See the map in the workbook.)
- The Promised Land in which the story of Joshua takes place was located west of the Dead Sea and the Jordan River and up to the Sea of Galilee.
- This is a book that brings to life the words of God in Zechariah 4:6: "Not by might nor by power, but by My Spirit ..."
  - ~ God would go <u>before</u> the Israelites, and it would be God Who would <u>ensure</u> their victory.

JOSHUA
Theme: Land Conquered

<u>REVIEW:</u> **Joshua, the Man**
- ¤ First introduced in the book of Exodus.
- ¤ Appointed by Moses as a general to lead a battle against the Amalekites (Exodus 17:9)
- ¤ Became a prominent figure as Moses' personal assistant, accompanying Moses when he went up on the mountain or to the tabernacle to meet with God.
- ¤ Under Moses' tutelage, God trained Joshua to become a great leader.
- ¤ He was from the tribe of Ephraim.
- ¤ One of the twelve spies Moses originally sent into the land.
  - ~ His heart was totally devoted to God.
  - ~ While ten of his fellow spies were afraid and refused to go into the land, Joshua, along with Caleb, encouraged the people to move forward and take the land. They knew God was with them and that He would ensure their victory.
- ¤ Joshua's faith made him an exceptional man.

⇨ **Joshua, whose name means "Jehovah is salvation," exhibited a Christ-like character in how he lived a life of devotion and obedience to God.**

> **NOTE:** It is worth mentioning that Scripture does not report Joshua committing any acts of sin.
> - ◆ Other great leaders had times when they missed the mark.
>   - ~ Abraham's fear led him to send his wife to a harem. (Genesis 12:11–20)
>   - ~ Moses hit the rock instead of speaking to it. (Numbers 20:1–13)
> - ◆ However, Joshua was not a perfect man, as all have sinned and fall short of the glory of God. (Romans 3:23)

⇨ **The purpose of Joshua is to tell the history of the Israelites conquering and dividing the land among the twelve tribes and then settling it.**

I.   THE ISRAELITES <u>ENTERED</u> THE PROMISED LAND (JOSHUA 1–5)

- ▪ The first five chapters of Joshua deal with the Israelites entering the Promised Land.
- ▪ As the book of Joshua opens, Moses had just died, and the people were located on the edge of the land of Canaan. They were camped on the east side of the Jordan River, which separated them from the Canaanites.

JOSHUA
Theme: Land Conquered

A. God gave a <u>CHARGE</u> to Joshua. (Joshua 1)

- God gave a charge to Joshua to cross the Jordan and get the people ready for battle. God was going to give the Israelites the land He had promised them.
- The charge was:

✝ **Joshua 1:8** "This book of the law shall not depart from your mouth, but you shall meditate on it day and night, so that you may be careful to do according to all that is written in it; for then you will make your way prosperous, and then you will have success."

- The "book of the law" that God was referring to was the Pentateuch, the first five books of the Bible.

> ★ **TEACHING TIP:**
>
> *In this passage, we see how the words Moses had written in the Pentateuch were given God's stamp of approval as holding full authority! We also see that God wanted Joshua to know that the book also held secrets to military success and national prosperity.*

- The Israelites were motivated to be fearless for one reason: ***God was with them.***

✝ **Joshua 1:9** "Have I not commanded you? Be strong and courageous! Do not tremble or be dismayed, for the Lord your God is with you wherever you go."

- They were going to face incredible battles with enemies far more skilled in warfare and greater in number.

⇨ **God commanded them to be men of courage because His power was enough for them.**

> **NOTE:** We need to always be mindful that the Word of God holds the secret to man's relationship with God:
> - It gives clear guidelines (instructions) or commands on how to behave because living in holiness does not come "natural" to us.
> - God is clear regarding obedience and what it is.
> - He is also clear on how to succeed with God and man.
>
> Christians are not promised "material" wealth for knowing and obeying God's Word; we are promised "spiritual" blessings and a deeper relationship with God.
> - The Word defines what sin is and the consequences of choosing to disobey.
>   - For example, sin such as coveting, anger, or jealousy may lead to mental and/or emotional bondage.
> - The Word states that the only way to live is in obedience to the Lord, which brings spiritual blessings.

JOSHUA
Theme: Land Conquered

****

❋ **ILLUSTRATION:** The world is full of mayhem, war, murder, and strife causing many today to live enslaved to fear. As a young woman, Patsy was brutally assaulted by a masked man who broke into her apartment just weeks before her wedding day. For over ten years, the trauma of that event left her living in a prison of fear from which she was unable to break free. Then a friend invited her to a Bible study that opened up the Word of God to her. Patsy soon received Christ as her Lord and Savior. It was when she read the book of Joshua that she realized God was commanding her to be a woman of courage. A word study on fear convinced her that this was a sin problem and that God had the key to setting her free. Through weeks of prayer and study, Patsy gradually began to trust God for her very life. The Bible did not promise that all would be well; but that, no matter what came into her life, God was with her and would give her the strength and grace to endure.

****

⇨ **The Word reveals God's power, character, holiness, grace, mercy , and love. It gives evidence of His presence, thus we <u>can</u> trust Him in times of sorrow or fear.**

> ❖ **APPLICATION:** What about you today?
>   ~ Do you believe that God is with you wherever you go?

⇨ **God's Word still holds power today and points to the All-Present Father Who can break down any stronghold, such as fear, anger, bitterness, lust, etc.**

B. Joshua sent out two <u>SPIES</u>. (Joshua 2)

▪ God gave Joshua a charge and then Joshua sent out two spies.

> **NOTE:** In Numbers, Moses sent out twelve spies to look over the land.
> ◆ Joshua had learned critical lessons from Moses' approach and chose a different tactic.
>   ~ Instead of twelve men, Joshua chose two men to spy out the land.
>   ~ He also chose not to inform the people of these men and their mission.
> ◆ Joshua's charge was to enter the land and that was his goal.
>   ~ He was not going to allow the people to once again be led astray by negative and exaggerated reports.

JOSHUA
Theme: Land Conquered

Joshua 2:1-7

- The two spies first went to Jericho.
- The king of Jericho learned of their presence and realized they were the enemy who had come to see how well the city was fortified, so he tried to capture them.
- Rahab, a prostitute, also learned of the two spies' presence in Jericho and assisted them by hiding them in her home, an act that put both her family and herself at risk of being killed for treason.

Joshua 2:8–21

- Rahab had come to believe that the Israelites' God was the one true God.

> ★ **TEACHING TIP:**
>
> *It is important to understand Rahab's heart and actions! She believed in God, thus was willing to put everything on the line for Him!*

- She shared with the spies that she had heard what their God had done in drying up the water of the Red Sea, and her heart had melted for she knew He was the God of heaven and earth.
- She begged them to remember her when the Israelites entered and destroyed the city.

⇨ **Rahab serves as an example of faith and courage for those who, out of fear, would be tempted to deny the Lord in the face of danger.**

- The spies returned to the other side of the Jordan and gave a good report to Joshua.

Joshua 3

- The people were ready to take the land, but there was one hurdle to overcome—the Jordan River!
  - ~ It also was a time of year when the river was at its highest.

> **NOTE:** In reality it would seem impossible for 2½ million people to cross the river at this time.
> - ◆ Yet it does not appear that anyone was concerned, as there was no grumbling!
> - ◆ Instead, they trusted God would get them across the Jordan River.

- God instructed Joshua to tell the priests to take the Ark of the Covenant and put their toes in the water.

- When the priests did, God parted the waters and the river stopped flowing fifteen miles upstream.
- Also, the riverbed was dry so they could walk across without sinking into the mud. Only God can do this!

★ **TEACHING TIP:**

Why fifteen miles? That much room was needed to get the 2½ million people across the river safely. We serve a God of details!

C. God parted the <u>JORDAN</u> River, and the Israelites crossed over. (Joshua 3–4)

> **NOTE:** The map in the workbook shows the Jordan River, Jericho, and Gilgal.
> - The Israelites started on the east side of the Jordan River.
> - They crossed at its mouth at the top of the Dead Sea.

- They then went into the land and passed Jericho.
- Jericho had a wall around it that stood thirty feet high.
- The people in Jericho knew that the enemy, the Israelites, had entered the land.
- The Israelites camped at Gilgal, which was only a few miles away.

Joshua 4

- Gilgal was the Israelites' home base.
    - ~ The warriors would leave Gilgal, go out and fight a battle, and then return.
    - ~ It was a place for the warriors to rest, be refreshed, regroup, and strategize.

Joshua 5

- The first action that was taken involved circumcising the men.
    - ~ The men who left Egypt as slaves were probably circumcised, but no one had been circumcised for at least forty years.
    - ~ All those born in the wilderness, which was this group, had to be circumcised.
    - ~ Circumcision was a mandatory sign of their covenant with God.

★ **TEACHING TIP:**

One would think that the people immediately began sharpening their swords to prepare for their conquest of the land. But that is <u>not</u> what happened. Instead, the people prepared for battle by ensuring they had a right relationship with God!

JOSHUA
Theme: Land Conquered

> **NOTE:** Consider this scenario!
> - When a grown man was circumcised, he was basically helpless for approximately three days.
> - The enemy is just a short distance away from where the Israelites were camped, yet these men had faith in God and followed through with this procedure.
> - They trusted in God's protection and kept their eyes on God and not on the enemy.

⇨ **These were men of courage and deep faith. They re-established the covenant in obedience and trust.**

- Next, they celebrated Passover.
  - ~ Passover had not been celebrated for forty years.
  - ~ In obedience to God, they had a great celebration.
- The day after this celebration, the manna ceased, and the people ate the fruit of the land.
- For forty years God had provided food and water. Now there was so much abundance of food in the land that manna was no longer necessary.
- The people were now prepared to take the land.
- But something unusual happened—Joshua saw a man standing nearby with a sword drawn!

D. Joshua <u>WORSHIPED</u> the captain of the Lord's host. (Joshua 5)

✝ **Joshua 5:13–15** "Now it came about when Joshua was by Jericho, that he lifted up his eyes and looked, and behold, a man was standing opposite him with his sword drawn in his hand, and Joshua went to him and said to him, 'Are you for us or for our adversaries?' He said, 'No; rather I indeed come now as captain of the host of the Lord.' And Joshua fell on his face to the earth, and bowed down, and said to him, 'What has my lord to say to his servant?' The captain of the Lord's host said to Joshua, 'Remove your sandals from your feet, for the place where you are standing is holy.' And Joshua did so."

> **NOTE:** When was the last time that we heard this phrase?
> - It occurred when Moses saw the burning bush and approached it.
> - Moses heard God say, "Do not come near here; remove your sandals from your feet, for the place on which you are standing is holy ground." (Exodus 3:5)
> - Moses obeyed, as did Joshua.

JOSHUA
Theme: Land Conquered

II. THE ISRAELITES <u>CONQUERED</u> THE PROMISED LAND. (JOSHUA 6–12)

- Joshua and his men were warriors who were ready for battle.
- The captain of the Lord of hosts gave Joshua instructions that were very unusual.
  - ~ The army was to march around the wall once a day, then return to Gilgal.
  - ~ Seven priests were to carry the ark of God around the wall while blowing the trumpets of rams' horns. This was to be done once a day. The warriors were to remain silent.
  - ~ The army and the priests were to do this for six days.
  - ~ On the seventh day, the priests were to blow the trumpets and the warriors were to shout.

> ★ **TEACHING TIP:**
>
> *Knowing that the Israelites faced a mighty enemy, this does not sound like a successful military strategy that will win a battle.*

- The warriors went to Jericho and obeyed every instruction that God gave.
- On the seventh day, they marched around the wall seven times and, when they heard the trumpets of rams' horns, they shouted, and the walls came down just as God had promised!
- When the walls came down, they entered Jericho and experienced a great victory.
- Everyone was killed as God commanded, except for one family—Rahab's! They were saved just as the spies had promised her.

A. God gave the Israelites victory at <u>JERICHO</u>. (Joshua 6)

⇨ **The Israelites obeyed God, and He gave them the city.**

B. Because of disobedience, the Israelites were disciplined at <u>AI</u>. (Joshua 7)

- The Israelites were now full of confidence as they had seen great things that God had done.
- The second city they were to conquer was Ai.
- They looked over the land and decided that approximately 30,000 warriors could go in and defeat this city. They were sure of victory, but something went terribly wrong, and they were routed from there.
  - ~ They saw that the enemy was more powerful than they were.
  - ~ In confusion, the warriors ran back to Gilgal with the news that they had lost thirty-six men.

- A greater confusion, however, set in as they had been assured of victory. Where was God? Why had He forsaken them?
  - ~ Joshua and the elders went before the Lord, fell on their faces and begged God to help them understand what had happened. They poured out their fear and bewilderment before Him.

> ❖ **APPLICATION:** Joshua and the elders did not run around in confusion, speculating about what had happened. Instead, they went straight to the One Who could answer their questions.
>
> ⇨ **Where do you run when events in life do not make sense?**

Joshua 7:9

- **Joshua asked**: "Lord, what will You do for Your great name?"

Joshua 7:10–13

- **God Answered:** There was sin within their own camp, and, as long as there was sin in the camp, the Israelites would not have victory.

> ★ **TEACHING TIP:**
> *Joshua is basically wrestling with and asking this: "What would be said of God by the enemies if He now allowed Israel to be destroyed?"*

Joshua 7:14–23

- **Sin Exposed**:
  - ~ Achan, who had been in Jericho, had taken gold, shekels, and an elaborate mantle from the conquered city, and he took them back to the camp.
  - ~ God had made it clear in the taking of Jericho that the spoils of the city were His.
    - * The people were to bring nothing back for themselves.
    - * The gold, silver, bronze, and iron were holy and were to go into the treasury of the Lord.
    - * Jericho was to be the first fruits, devoted to the Lord. The other cities' spoils would belong to the people.
  - ~ Achan knew this, yet still took items for himself.

Joshua 7:24–26

- **Sin Addressed:**
  - ~ In obedience to God, Joshua and all of the people took Achan and his family (along with all of their belongings <u>including</u> the forbidden spoil of Jericho) out of the camp.

~ Achan and his family were stoned, then burned along with all that had brought sin into the camp.

~ The camp was then cleansed.

Joshua 8

- The warriors went to Ai again, and this time they were victorious. They conquered the city and brought all the spoil back to camp.
    - ~ God had asked for the first fruits and Jericho was the first fruits that was set aside for the Lord.
    - ~ After Jericho, the people would get the spoils and even more as the story unfolds.

> **NOTE:** Have you ever done something that you thought God would not know about? He knows! Because of one man's sin, the entire camp suffered. This is a good lesson for us to remember.
> - When one person <u>chooses</u> to continue in sin, it brings pain to others.
> - If there is sin in the camp—in your home—everyone in the family suffers. And sometimes those in our communities and neighborhoods suffer as well.

> ❖ **APPLICATION:** We do not sin "in a vacuum." When we <u>choose</u> to sin, that choice often has far-reaching, damaging, consequences.
> - ~ How can you teach this truth to your family?
> - ~ Are you dealing with your own sin?

⇨ **Sin is a choice—to obey or disobey God is a choice. The choices we make impact others. Consequences from sin cannot be avoided.**

C. The Israelites approach to Canaan was <u>DIVIDE</u> and conquer. (Joshua 9–12)

- They came into the center of Canaan and began to take the cities.

> **NOTE:** The cities of Canaan were not as barbaric as one might have assumed.
> - The houses were very well laid out with paved floors.
> - Most of the cities had their own king and their own warriors.

- Canaan was not a united nation but consisted of many smaller communities, each with their own ruler, which resulted in battles taking place between the various cities. The warriors were in good fighting shape and well-versed in war.
- The Israelites had to conquer each and every city—one at a time.
  - ~ They began by taking out the cities in the center of the country.
  - ~ They then conquered cities in the south and then the north.
- ¤ Their military strategy was simple: divide and conquer.

REVIEW:

¤ God said in Deuteronomy 6:10–12 – "Then it shall come about when the Lord your God brings you into the land which He swore to your fathers, Abraham, Isaac and Jacob, to give you, great and splendid cities which you did not build, and houses full of all good things which you did not fill, and hewn cisterns which you did not dig, vineyards and olive trees which you did not plant ... then watch yourself, that you do not forget the Lord ..."

> **NOTE:** Almost all of the battles were fought <u>outside</u> of the cities.
> - ♦ The Israelites would lure the enemy warriors out of their city and defeat them there.
> - ♦ Then the Israelites would return to Gilgal to regroup.

¤ Fighting outside of the cities resulted in the cities remaining intact.
  - ~ The Israelites were able to keep the houses, the vineyards, and the olive trees that had been planted and the wells that had been dug.
  - ~ The Israelites did not have to do anything but move in!

✝ **Joshua 24:13** "I gave you a land on which you had not labored, and cities which you had not built, and you have lived in them; you are eating of vineyards and olive groves which you did not plant."

⇨ **God had made a promise to Israel in Deuteronomy and He fulfilled it here. When God says something, believe it because it will happen! God will bring it about.**

III. THE ISRAELITES <u>DIVIDED</u> THE LAND AMONG THE TWELVE TRIBES. (JOSHUA 13–24)

- It took the Israelites seven years to conquer the land.
- The next step was to divide the land among the twelve tribes who were the descendants of the twelve sons of Jacob.
  - ~ One son, Levi, did not get any land.

- ~ Joseph had two sons, Ephraim and Manasseh, and each became a tribe.
  - After the land was divided and settled, peace was experienced at last.

⇨ **God had promised Abraham (in Genesis) a people and a land. Here we see His promises fulfilled!**

- Each tribe was allotted a particular piece of land. The map in the workbook shows the divisions.
  - ~ Gad, Reuben and the ½ tribe of Manasseh received the land that was east of the Jordan River. That area was referred to as the Transjordan.
  - ~ The other tribes settled west of the Jordan River.
- Dividing the land took incredible organizational skills from the leaders; it also took a great amount of time. In fact, it would be eighteen years before this job was completed!

⇨ **There were two groups of people of special interest.**

A. The <u>GIBEONITES</u> were allowed to live among the Israelites. (Joshua 9)

- The Gibeonites were a people from a great city approximately six miles from Ai.
- They had heard about the Israelites and their God and were very afraid. Therefore, they hatched a plan of deceit.
  - ~ They dressed in old clothes and sandals and carried wine skins that were old.
  - ~ Their tactic was to appear as if they had traveled for months, if not years.
  - ~ They told the Israelites that they had traveled a long way and desired to make a covenant with the Israelites.

> **NOTE:** God had given clear instructions to the Israelites—that all the inhabitants of Canaan needed to be destroyed. They could make peace with more distant cities.
> ✝ **Deuteronomy 7:1–2** "When the Lord your God brings you into the land where you are entering to possess it, and clears away many nations before you … seven nations greater and stronger than you, and when the Lord your God delivers them before you and you defeat them, then you shall utterly destroy them. You shall make no covenant with them and show no favor to them."

> **NOTE:** God's instructions to the Israelites. (contd.)
> ✝ **Deuteronomy 20:10–15** "When you approach a city to fight against it, you shall offer it terms of peace. If it agrees to make peace with you and opens to you, then all the people who are found in it shall become your forced labor and shall serve you. However, if it does not make peace with you, but makes war against you, then you shall besiege it. When the Lord your God gives it into your hand, you shall strike all the men in it with the edge of the sword. Only the women and the children and the animals and all that is in the city, all its spoil, you shall take as booty for yourself; and you shall use the spoil of your enemies which the Lord your God has given you. Thus you shall do to all the cities that are very far from you, which are not of the cities of these nations nearby."

- Joshua and the elders believed the Gibeonites' lies that they had traveled from a far distance.
- Sadly, they made a covenant with the Gibeonites without ever consulting the Lord Who would have revealed the deceitful scheme being implemented.
- When the elders found out the truth of this deceit, the Gibeonites were allowed to live because of the covenant, but they became slaves.
  - ~ The Gibeonties had to hew the wood and draw the water—but they were alive.
  - ~ There is more about the Gibeonites in 2 Samuel 21:1–9.

B. The <u>LEVITES</u> received the sacrifice of God as their inheritance, not the land. (Joshua 21)

- The Levites did not receive a large piece of land in which the entire tribe would live as the other tribes.
- They were the spiritual leaders and one of their jobs was to teach the law to the people.
  - ~ If the Levites had all lived in a tribe together, there would not have been spiritual leadership throughout the land.
- The Levites were, instead, scattered and given cities and land for their gardens.

> ✱ **TEACHING TIP:**
>
> *It is believed that everyone in Israel lived within five to ten miles of a Levite who would provide spiritual direction and education.*

C. Joshua gave a final <u>CHARGE</u> to the people of Israel. (Joshua 22–24)

- At the end of the book Joshua gave a charge to his people:

JOSHUA
Theme: Land Conquered

✝ **Joshua 24:15** "If it is disagreeable in your sight to serve the Lord, choose for yourselves today whom you will serve … but as for me and my house, we will serve the Lord."

D. There are three burials at the end of Joshua. (Joshua 24:29–33)

1. JOSHUA

- The first burial was Joshua, who died at 110 years of age.
- He had served God faithfully to the end.
- He had seen God do mighty deeds and, although his responsibilities had been great and his life full of war, Joshua had clung with fervency to His God.
- Joshua knew God would be faithful and was trustworthy.

⇨ **To this day, Joshua is seen as one of the greatest leaders of all time.**

2. JOSEPH'S BONES

- The second burial involved Jacob's son, Joseph.
- This burial was strange, yet showed the commitment of the people to do what Joseph had requested over 400 years earlier.
- Joseph had asked that when the people came into the land that God had promised, they would bury his bones there. (Genesis 50:24-25)
    - ~ This required the people to carry his bones with them!
- Joseph had trusted that what God had promised, God would bring about.
    - ~ God had promised the people a land of their own, and Joseph wanted to be there with his people when that happened.
- The people, honoring Joseph's request, buried his bones in the Promised Land.

3. ELEAZAR

- The last burial that took place involved Eleazar, Aaron's son.
- After Aaron died, Eleazar became the high priest and took charge of the tabernacle and worship.
- Eleazar, as the High Priest, was the one who would go into the Holy of Holies once a year and offer sacrifices for the people.
- Like Joshua, Eleazar proved to be a man of great faith throughout his whole life.

⇨ **Joshua is called the book of conquest. God led the Israelites through the leadership of Joshua, a man who was wholeheartedly devoted and obedient to God.**

JOSHUA
Theme: Land Conquered

⇨ ## <u>PICTURES OF JESUS IN JOSHUA</u>

(1)   Jesus—the man with the drawn sword who spoke to Joshua at Jericho.

▪ Many scholars believe this man who spoke to Joshua before the battle of Jericho was Jesus.

▪ When God appeared in human form in the Old Testament, it is called a theophany, and it is believed to be Jesus.

▪ In 1 Corinthians, we are told that God gives us victory through our Lord Jesus Christ.

✝ **1 Corinthians 15:57** "... but thanks be to God, who gives us the victory through our Lord Jesus Christ."

⇨ **Here is the Lord Jesus Christ in the book of Joshua concealed, yet revealed. Amazing how God works!**

<u>FINAL THOUGHTS AND APPLICATION</u>

⌶ In the Old Testament, God gave His people a special land to call their own and to establish their nation.

⌶ Today, God has not promised believers land. He has promised us something much better in Jesus Christ.

✝ **Ephesians 2:19** "So then you are no longer strangers and aliens, but you are fellow citizens with the saints, and are of God's household..."

~ God is not bringing believers into a land—He is bringing us into His very household as His children. We are part of His family, His sons and daughters!

⌶ In total devotion to God, Joshua led the people by following God every step of the way.

~ He lived in obedience even when obeying God was difficult.

~ He sadly recognized that the Israelites were "prone to wander from the God they loved."

⇨ **Let's consider the charge that Joshua gave the Israelites—one that we should take seriously today: "Choose for yourselves today whom you will serve."**

⌶ This is a personal choice, but we learn from the book of Joshua that to choose to serve the Lord, as Joshua did, is by far the wisest choice we could and will ever make.

⇨ **Whom do you choose?**

❖ **<u>FINAL APPLICATION</u>: God's power easily defeats His children's foes. He is our defender, strength, comfort, hope, and security. In Him we take courage.**

JOSHUA REVIEW HELPS

1. What does the word *Pentateuch* mean?

2. What four big events took place within the first eleven chapters of Genesis?

3. What man did God choose to be the father of a great nation?

4. Name the Patriarchs.

5. At the end of Genesis, where is Jacob's family living?

6. How long were the Israelites in slavery in Egypt?

7. Who did God choose to lead the people out of slavery in Egypt?

8. How many plagues were there and who were they against?

9. Where did God take the people so He could teach and train them?

10. How many commandments did God write on tablets?

11. Where was the tabernacle located?

12. What instruction book did God give the Levites and Priests?

13. What was the way the Israelites could approach God? (through what method)

14. Why did the Israelites refuse to go into the Promised Land?

15. What was their punishment?

16. In what book are the three sermons recorded that Moses gave to the new generation just before he died?

17. In what book did Moses die?

18. Who took Moses' place of leadership?

19. Where were the Israelites at the end of the Pentateuch?

20. What is one thing you learned about God in these first five books of the Bible?

JOSHUA REVIEW HELPS

✧ **Name the book each of the following are in:**

Wandering in the wilderness

Restated the law

The flood

Slavery in Egypt

Sacrifices

Three sermons

Moses dies

Feasts and offerings

Arrived at Mt. Sinai

Tricked his father-in-law

Land and water parted

Talking donkey

Ten Commandments

Different languages began

Ten plagues

Sodom destroyed

Red Sea parts

Twelve spies

Priest's handbook

A whole generation dies within forty years

JOSHUA REVIEW HELPS
(Answers for Facilitators)

1. What does the word *Pentateuch* mean?
   Five books or scrolls
2. What four big events took place within the first eleven chapters of Genesis?
   Creation – Fall – Flood - Nations
3. What man did God choose to be the father of a great nation?
   Abraham
4. Name the Patriarchs.
   Abraham, Isaac, Jacob, Joseph
5. At the end of Genesis, where is Jacob's family living?
   Egypt
6. How long were the Israelites in slavery in Egypt?
   About 400 years
7. Who did God choose to lead the people out of slavery in Egypt?
   Moses
8. How many plagues were there and who were they against?
   Ten plagues against Egypt
9. Where did God take the people so He could teach and train them?
   Mt. Sinai
10. How many commandments did God write on tablets?
    Ten Commandments
11. Where was the tabernacle located?
    In the center of the camp
12. What instruction book did God give the Levites and Priests?
    Leviticus
13. What was the way the Israelites could approach God? (through what method)
    Sacrifice
14. Why did the Israelites refuse to go into the Promised Land?
    Afraid of the inhabitants
15. What was their punishment?
    Wandering forty years until the adult generation had died
16. In what book are the three sermons recorded that Moses gave to the new generation just before he died?
    Deuteronomy
17. In what book did Moses die?
    Deuteronomy
18. Who took Moses' place of leadership?
    Joshua
19. Where were the Israelites at the end of the Pentateuch?
    Eastern shore of the Jordan River in the land of Moab
20. What is one thing you learned about God in these first five books of the Bible?
    Varied answers

JOSHUA REVIEW HELPS
(Answers for Facilitators)

✧ **Name the book each of the following are in:**

Wandering in the wilderness	**NUMBERS**
Restated the law	**DEUTERONOMY**
The flood	**GENESIS**
Slavery in Egypt	**EXODUS**
Sacrifices	**LEVITICUS**
Three sermons	**DEUTERONOMY**
Moses dies	**DEUTERONOMY**
Feasts and offerings	**LEVITICUS**
Arrived at Mt. Sinai	**EXODUS**
Tricked his father-in-law	**GENESIS (JACOB)**
Land and water parted	**GENESIS**
Talking donkey	**NUMBERS**
Ten Commandments	**EXODUS**
Different languages began	**GENESIS**
Ten plagues	**EXODUS**
Sodom destroyed	**GENESIS**
Red Sea parts	**EXODUS**
Twelve spies	**NUMBERS**
Priest's handbook	**LEVITICUS**
A whole generation dies out	**NUMBERS**

JUDGES

Judges Ruled

In those days there was no king in Israel;
everyone did what was right in his own eyes.

Judges 21:25

SESSION SEVEN: JUDGES
Judges Ruled

✝ **Memory Verse:** *"In those days there was no king in Israel; everyone did what was right in his own eyes."* *(Judges 21:25)*

- **Introduction:** The story continues from the book of Joshua as the nation of Israel struggles to learn what it means to be a nation under God as their King. They were continually tempted by the worship of other gods as the land was never fully conquered and cleansed from the Canaanite influence. At least seven times the people turned from God, God brought another nation that oppressed the people, they repented and cried out to God for help and He rescued them again. This book covers about 340 years.

- **Oral Review:** Please refer to the **REVIEW Section** in the following Teaching Guide Outline.

- **Homework:** Review the homework from the book of Joshua. Key questions are:

    Questions on page 33–34
    Questions on page 37
    Questions on page 39
    Questions on page 42–43

- **Review Helps:** Written review is provided at the end of the teachers' presentation. (Optional and time permitting.)

- **Teacher Presentation over the Book of Judges**

- **Learning for Life Discussion questions:** You may choose to discuss all or just one or two of the questions on page 55.

- **Closing prayer**: Pray that each student would become aware of any sin cycle in their lives and would repent and ask God to give them victory as they surrender to His will.

JUDGES
Theme: Judges Ruled

TIMELINE AID FOR TEACHERS:

DIVISION ONE: The CAUSES of Israel's Failure

- **Judges 1**   Israel failed to rid the land of enemies
- **Judges 2**   Joshua died

                           The godly elders died

DIVISION TWO: The CYCLES of Israel's Failure

⇨ **Sin cycles: People rebelled > God rejected > People repented >**

       God rescued/judged > Rest

- **Judges 2:3–3:11**   Othniel
- **Judges 3:12–30**   Ehud
- **Judges 3:31**   Shamgar
- **Judges 4:1-5:31**   Deborah
- **Judges 6:1-7:25**   Gideon
- **Judges 8:33–9:57**   Abimelech
- **Judges 10:1–2**   Tola
- **Judges 10:3–4**   Jair
- **Judges 10:6–11**   Jephthah
- **Judges 12:8–10**   Ibzan
- **Judges 12:11–2**   Elon
- **Judges 12:13–15**   Abdon
- **Judges 13:1–16:30**   Samson

DIVISION THREE: The CONSEQUENCES of Israel's Failure

⇨ **The consequences of not allowing God to be king were:**

- **Judges 17–18**   Idolatry
- **Judges 19**   Immorality
- **Judges 20–21**   Civil War

JUDGES
[Judges Ruled]

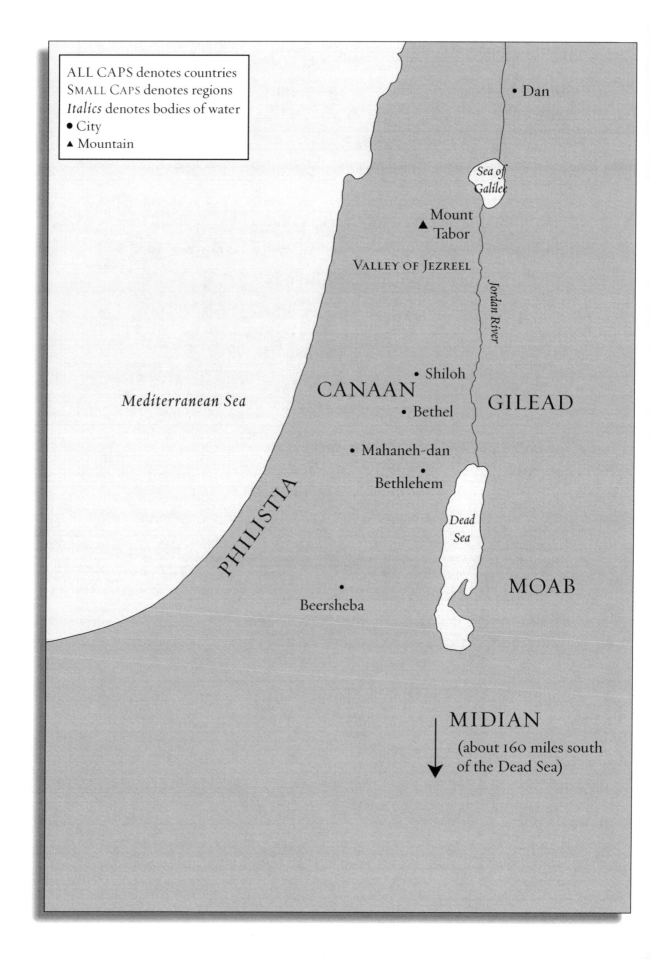

ALL CAPS denotes countries
SMALL CAPS denotes regions
Italics denotes bodies of water
● City
▲ Mountain

• Dan

Sea of Galilee

▲ Mount Tabor

VALLEY OF JEZREEL

Jordan River

Mediterranean Sea

• Shiloh

CANAAN

GILEAD

• Bethel

• Mahaneh-dan

Bethlehem

Dead Sea

PHILISTIA

MOAB

•
Beersheba

MIDIAN
(about 160 miles south
of the Dead Sea)

JUDGES
Theme: Judges Ruled

THE BASICS:

⇨ **Who: The Author:** Is Anonymous (the Talmud suggests Samuel)
        Main Characters: Israel's judges such as Deborah, Gideon, Samson
⇨ **What:** Everyone did what was right in his own eyes
⇨ **When:** 1390-1050 B.C. Judges covers the 330 to 340 years between the conquest of the land and Israel's monarchy.
⇨ **Where:** In the Promised Land of Israel
⇨ **Why:** Shows the consequences of sin

MEMORY VERSE: *"In those days there was no king in Israel; everyone did what was right in his own eyes." Judges 21:25*

****

REVIEW:

⌘ The first seventeen books of the Bible are ***Old Testament History*** books.

The Pentateuch

⌘ The first five books were called the ***Pentateuch***, which gives a foundation for the rest of the Bible.

~ God is the creator of everything; man was made in His image; through Adam's rebellion sin entered the world.

~ God raised up Abraham and gave him three promises: (1) a people/nation; (2) land of their own; and (3) a descendant who would be a blessing to the world.

~ In Egypt, Abraham's descendants grew from seventy to approximately 2½ million people. Moses led them out of slavery, and God began to train the people through moral and civil laws and laws of worship.

~ The people rebelled and, as a consequence, they wandered forty years in the wilderness until that generation died.

~ God raised up another generation who loved and obeyed God.

⌘ At the end of the Pentateuch, the people were ready to enter and take the land God had promised them.

Joshua

⌘ The book of Joshua is the first of the *Kingdom books in the Old Testament.*

⌘ Joshua was appointed by God to be the leader to replace Moses.

⌘ God parted the waters of the Jordan River, as He had done with the Red Sea. The people were able to walk safely across into the Promised Land.

JUDGES
Theme: Judges Ruled

¤ The people experienced victory in their first battle, which was against Jericho. They were victorious because they had obeyed God's instructions, which required their absolute faith in His power.

¤ The book covers twenty-five years describing how the Israelites conquered and divided the land among the tribes.

¤ Joshua not only led the Israelites into the Promised Land, but also led them in their spiritual walk with God.

****

❋ **ILLUSTRATION:** A husband and his wife felt the pressure of financial bondage as they were greatly in debt. The husband received a generous bonus at work, and they determined to pay the debt off. They went from store to store paying off all that was owed. They felt great freedom in not being in the bondage of debt. Soon after they paid their last bill, they saw a sign: Sale of the Year! They could not pass up such a fabulous "sale." And how did they buy those new items? With a credit card. They went back into debt once more! We often repeat poor choices because we do not learn the lesson from the consequences.

****

OVERVIEW:

- The Israelites did the same thing with sin. They continually found themselves owing a sin debt.

- Judges is about a people who did what seemed right in their own eyes, regardless of what God said.

- Judges is also a book of hope and encouragement for in it we see that time and time again God forgave the Israelites once they repented of their sin.

- After conquering the land, Joshua reminded them to:

☦ **Joshua 24:15** " ... choose for yourselves today whom you will serve: whether the gods which your fathers served which were beyond the River, or the gods of the Amorites in whose land you are living; but as for me and my house, we will serve the Lord."

- The people responded to Joshua:

☦ **Joshua 24:16, 24** "Far be it from us that we should forsake the Lord to serve other gods ... we will serve the Lord our God and we will obey His voice."

> ❋ **TEACHING TIP:**
>
> *Good intentions are not enough and often people do not learn from their past mistakes, but instead repeat them. The book of Judges will amplify this truth, for just as the couple in our illustration quickly fell back into debt, the Israelites repeatedly fell back into sin.*

JUDGES
Theme: Judges Ruled

- The people had good intentions.

⇨ **The people had resoundingly promised to follow and obey God in the book of Joshua; yet in Judges, even though God was to be their king, they refused to honor Him as such.**

- Judges, with striking clarity, shows the consequences of choices, especially when man does what seems right in his own eyes but, in fact, is living apart from God.
- Judges takes place in Israel (formerly Canaan) after the people conquered the land and before Saul became the first king and the twelve tribes became one kingdom. This time period covered approximately 340 years (1390-1050 B.C.).
- During the time of the judges there were twelve small states or family territories. Some events in Judges may have taken place simultaneously.
  - ~ When a judge ruled in one part of the country, there could have also been a judge ruling in another territory.

⇨ **The purpose of the book Judges is to show Israel's 340 year history of living as a theocracy and their repeated sin cycles.**

- There are three divisions in the book of Judges:
  - ~ **Judges 1–2**   The **CAUSES** of Israel's failure
  - ~ **Judges 3-16**   The **CYCLES** of Israel's failure
  - ~ **Judges 17-21**   The **CONSEQUENCES** of Israel's failure

I.   THE <u>CAUSES</u> OF ISRAEL'S FAILURE (JUDGES 1-2)

- Judges begins with the people living in the land.

A. Joshua died but his godly influence lived on through surviving <u>ELDERS</u>.
<u>Judges 1:1–8</u>

- After Joshua died, the people continued to follow God because of Joshua's influence over the elders.
- The Lord was with Judah so they were victorious in temporarily capturing Jerusalem and the hill country.
  - ~ God gave them victory over the Canaanites and the Perizzites.
- When the Israelites looked to God, they had victory after victory, just as they had when Joshua was alive.
- God promised to give them the land, but He clearly also instructed them to:
  - ~ Tear down the altars to pagan gods anywhere they were found.
  - ~ Drive the heathens out of the land.

JUDGES
Theme: Judges Ruled

- The Israelites did not obey God <u>completely</u>:
  - ~ They did not drive out the Jebusites who lived in Jerusalem. (Judges 1:21)
  - ~ They did not drive the Canaanites out of the land; instead they put them into forced labor.
  - ~ Seven times in Chapter One, the Scriptures states, "they did not drive out the inhabitants of the land."

⇨ **Partial obedience is disobedience, and there are consequences!**

> **NOTE:** What was the devastating consequence of not removing the enemy from the land as God had instructed?
> - ◆ The wicked influence of the enemy was allowed to flourish.
> - ◆ The impact was two-fold on the Israelites:
>   1. It drew them <u>to</u> idol worship.
>   2. It drew them <u>away from</u> the one true God.

B. The Israelites rebelled against God and worshiped <u>IDOLS</u>.

- Soon Israel began to do evil in God's sight, worshiping the gods of the people around them.
- Obedience to God had brought victory but, as the influence of the heathen people became stronger, the victories were fewer and fewer, and the people turned away from God.

⇨ **God had called the Israelites to be holy—set apart—but the Israelites began to blend in with the current culture and look like its participants, instead of God's children.**

C. The elders died and the new generation did not know God nor the <u>WORK</u> He had done for Israel.

✝ **Judges 2:7–12** "The people served the Lord all the days of Joshua, and all the days of the elders who survived Joshua, who had seen all the great work of the Lord which He had done for Israel. Then Joshua the son of Nun, the servant of the Lord, died at the age of one hundred and ten. … All that generation also were gathered to their fathers; and there arose another generation after them who did not know the Lord, nor yet the work which He had done for Israel. Then the sons of Israel did evil in the sight of the Lord and served the Baals, and they forsook the Lord, the God of their fathers, who had brought them out of the land of Egypt, and followed other gods from among the gods ..."

> **NOTE:** It is important to ask "why." Why didn't this generation know about God? Two reasons:
> 1. They had not witnessed for themselves the work God had done for Israel.
> 2. They were not told about Him or taught His Word
>
> ◆ Remember—in Deuteronomy, God had commanded the people to share their experiences and teach God's Word as a habit of their lives to their children!

⇨ **The people rebelled against God.**

D. God's hand was against the Israelites and they were oppressed and <u>DISCIPLINED</u> by other nations.

✝ **Judges 2:14–15** "The anger of the Lord burned against Israel, and He gave them into the hands of plunderers who plundered them; and He sold them into the hands of their enemies around them, so that they could no longer stand before their enemies. Wherever they went, the hand of the Lord was against them for evil, as the Lord had spoken and as the Lord had sworn to them, so that they were severely distressed."

> **★ TEACHING TIP:**
> *Do you recall what God had told the Israelites about the consequences of obedience and disobedience? One brought blessings—the other curses. (Deuteronomy 28)*

- God allowed foreign nations to have victory over the Israelites, for the Israelite's rebellion was evil in His sight. Thus the Israelites were:
  ~ Plundered (which means raided and robbed)
  ~ Sold into the hands of the enemies (which means enslaved)
  ~ Unable to stand before their enemies (which means defeated)

> **★ TEACHING TIP:**
> *What a contrast to the victories against the enemies under the leadership of Joshua who had been faithful to God!*

- God rejected Israel and allowed the enemy to come in and oppress the people.

✝ **Judges 3:3–4** "These nations are: the five lords of the Philistines and all the Canaanites and the Sidonians and the Hivites who lived in Mount Lebanon, from Mount Baal-hermon as far as Lebo-hamath. They were for testing Israel, to find out if they would obey the commandments of the Lord, which He had commanded their fathers through Moses."

- God used these enemy nations to test Israel. What was the test?
  - ~ To see if the people would come back and obey the commandments of the Lord, which He had commanded their fathers through Moses

E. The sin <u>CYCLES</u> followed this pattern: Israel rebelled – God rejected – Israel repented – God rescued – Israel rested.

F. There are <u>SEVEN</u> cycles of sin in the book of Judges.

- The five "Rs" of the cycles of sin were:
  1) The people would **REBEL** against God.

  2) God would **REJECT** them, allowing enemies to attack and oppress them.

  3) When life became too difficult, the people cried out to God and **REPENTED.**

  4) God heard their cries and would send a **RESCUER** or judge to save them.

  5) And the land would have **REST**—*u*ntil the people repeated the cycle again.

II. THE <u>CYCLES</u> OF ISRAEL'S FAILURE. (JUDGES 3–16)

⇨ **The word *judge* in Hebrew means "ruler, deliverer, or savior."**

- The judges God raised up after each of the seven sin cycles were ordinary men (and a woman) who God changed into extraordinary people to be military and political leaders.
- The judges delivered, liberated, and saved Israel.
- Though all of the judges were important, three stand out: Deborah, Gideon, and Samson.
- Before Deborah there had been three judges: Othniel, Ehud, and Shamgar.
  - ~ All had struck down the enemies and had saved Israel.
  - ~ However, after each one died, the sin cycle would begin again.
- After the judge Shamgar, the Israelites were oppressed for twenty years. The people lived in fear of their powerful enemy, Sisera, who was well-equipped with 900 chariots.
- The people needed to be rescued, and God called Deborah.

⇨ **Deborah was a heroine in a land that needed hope.**

JUDGES
Theme: Judges Ruled

A. Though a woman, <u>DEBORAH</u> led Israel to victory against Jabin, king of Canaan.

<u>Judges 4:1–23, 5:31b</u>

- The third sin cycle begins in Judges 4:
  - ~ The people **rebelled:** "The sons of Israel again did evil in the sight of the Lord …" (Judges 4:1)
  - ~ God **rejected** them: "And the Lord sold them into the hand of Jabin king of Canaan …" (Judges 4:2)
  - ~ The people **repented**: "The sons of Israel cried to the Lord; for he [Sisera, the commander of Jabin's army] had nine hundred iron chariots, and he oppressed the sons of Israel severely for twenty years." (Judges 4:3)
  - ~ God sent a **rescuer**: "Now Deborah, a prophetess … was judging Israel at that time." (Judges 4:4)
  - ~ The land had **rest**: "And the land was undisturbed for forty years." (Judges 5:31)

- Deborah was the only woman in all of Scripture that God put in a position of leadership in time of war.

⇨ **God uses whomever He chooses, when they are willing.**

<u>Judges 4:4–10</u>

- Deborah held court under a tree and all of the sons of Israel came to her for judgment.
- God told Deborah to have ten thousand men march to Mount Tabor and God assured their victory.
- She called for Barak, one of the generals in the army, and told him what God had said.
- Barak agreed to the plan only **if** Deborah would go with him, and she agreed.
- Deborah told Barak that he would not receive the honor of this victory; instead the honor would go to another woman.

<u>Judges 4:17-23</u>

- That other woman was Jael, who did receive the victory.
- God used Jael to defeat Sisera by driving a tent peg into his temple!

⇨ **There are lessons to be learned and applied from the story of Deborah:**

1. Women are uniquely made to be uniquely used by God.

- Though God has made women different, He delights in using both men and women.
- We face battles today: they are raging in our homes, neighborhoods, schools, workplaces, and the nations.

- In our own individual and personal situations, God is not necessarily looking for our ability, but He IS looking for our availability.

⇨ **God makes us able—He equips us to do whatever He has called us to do.**

2. Under Deborah's rule Israel enjoyed peace for <u>FORTY</u> years.

- Deborah had influence: she was a wife, a judge, and a prophetess (which means that she was an inspired speaker or one who spoke for God).
- Like Deborah, we have been given spheres of influence: in our homes, neighborhoods, workplace, children's schools, churches, and even in sports we may play. In all of these various arenas, we have opportunities to make a difference.

⇨ **God has work for all of us to do. What has He created you to do?**

- Another sin cycle began in Chapter Six.

✞ **Judges 6:1, 5-6** "Then the sons of Israel did what was evil in the sight of the Lord; and the Lord gave them into the hands of Midian seven years ... For they [the Midianites] would come up with their livestock and their tents, they would come in like locusts for number, both they and their camels were innumerable; and they came into the land to devastate it. So Israel was brought very low because of Midian, and the sons of Israel cried to the Lord."

- Once more Israel rebelled, and God rejected them by sending in an enemy.
- And once more when life became too difficult, Israel cried out to God and repented.

B. Though a man with little courage, <u>GIDEON</u> led Israel to victory against the Midianites.

- God can even use the fearful. The judge He chose this time was Gideon.
- The Midianites were like bandits in the hills.
  - ~ They would swoop down and destroy the produce and flocks, leaving no sustenance for the people.
- The Israelites were living in caves and were very frightened by the Midianites.
- In fact, Gideon hid in a wine press to thresh his wheat, because he knew if he threshed in the open, the Midianites would come and take his food.

⇨ **Gideon was hiding from the enemy when the angel of the Lord appeared.**

⇨ **There are lessons to be learned and applied from the story of Gideon:**

JUDGES
Theme: Judges Ruled

1. God knows who we are, and He knows what we can become.

✞ **Judges 6:12** The angel of the Lord appeared to him and said to him, "The Lord is with you, O valiant warrior."

- Do you think Gideon saw himself as a warrior, much less a valiant one? Gideon was hiding from the enemy and not acting like a warrior in any sense of the word!

⇨ **God knew not only who Gideon was at that point—but who and what Gideon could become with God's power.**

❖ **APPLICATION:** This is true for each person doing this study.
  ~ God knows you, and He knows your potential in His power and strength.

- Gideon's response to the angel of the Lord is found in Chapter 6:13.

✞ **Judges 6:13** "Then Gideon said to him, 'O my lord, if the Lord is with us, why then has all this happened to us? And where are all His miracles which our fathers told us about, saying, 'Did not the Lord bring us up from Egypt?' But now the Lord has abandoned us and given us into the hand of Midian.'"

- Gideon's response reflects a fearful heart:
  ~ The angel of the Lord had said, "God is with you." Gideon responded, "IF God is with us …"
  ~ Gideon's focus was on his circumstances NOT the call from God.
  ~ This reminds us of the ten spies who saw "giants" in the land as bigger than almighty God. (Numbers 13:31-33)
  ~ Gideon's perspective was one of defeat as he stood before the angel of God (Jesus).

2. God is not looking for my ability but for my availability.

- God told Gideon to go and deliver Israel because He, God, had sent Him.
- Gideon's response, once again, does not reflect valiant behavior, but instead varied excuses:
  ~ His family was not important. In other words, he did not have the "status" to lead.
  ~ He was the youngest in his family. In other words, he was too young to lead.

JUDGES
Theme: Judges Ruled

❖ **APPLICATION:** Can you relate?

~ Have you ever responded to God with excuses when you felt Him calling you to do something? I am too young. I am too old. I am too busy. I am too unqualified.

~ When we answer God with excuses, it is as if we are telling Him that we do not believe He is able to do what He says He will do.

✝ **Judges 6:16–17** "But the Lord said to him, 'Surely I will be with you, and you shall defeat Midian as one man.' So Gideon said to Him, 'If now I have found favor in Your sight, then show me a sign that it is You who speak with me.'"

- **God's Response:** "I will be with you, Gideon. I will enable you in this calling."
- **Gideon's Response:** One of doubt—he wanted a "sign."

Judges 6:19–22

- Gideon prepared a sacrifice. The angel of the Lord touched the meat and bread and fire sprang up from the rock and consumed the sacrifice.
- Gideon knew then that the angel of the Lord was God, "Alas, O Lord God! For now I have seen the angel of the Lord face to face."

> ★ **TEACHING TIP:**
> *Gideon believed that his life was in peril once he recognized the divinity of the angel of the Lord. He knew that no one could see the face of God and live.*

✝ **Judges 6:23** "The Lord said to him, 'Peace to you, do not fear; you shall not die.'"

✝ **Judges 6:36–37** "Then Gideon said to God, 'If You will deliver Israel through me, as You have spoken, behold, I will put a fleece of wool on the threshing floor. If there is dew on the fleece only, and it is dry on all the ground, then I will know that You will deliver Israel through me, as You have spoken.'"

> ★ **TEACHING TIP:**
> *Don't miss the fact that Gideon knew what God had said. He knew the will of God for his life, BUT Gideon wanted to know if God really meant it!*

⇨ **Gideon was not only a man of great fears—but also a man of great doubts.**

❖ **APPLICATION:** Again—can you relate to Gideon?

~ You know God's word, and you know His will ... BUT ...?

- God graciously answered Gideon's doubts by making the fleece wet one time and dry another.
- By this act, God was assuring Gideon that He indeed would be with Gideon and would use Gideon to deliver Israel.

> ★ **TEACHING TIP:**
> *We see how merciful God was to Gideon, but we must realize that it is not good to doubt what God has clearly said.*

3. Under Gideon's rule Israel enjoyed peace for <u>FORTY</u> years.

<u>Judges 7</u>
- In spite of Gideon's doubts, he was used by God in a mighty way.
- God told Gideon to gather an army of 32,000 men. God then instructed Gideon to reduce the number to 300 men. Such a drastic reduction would prevent them from becoming prideful in their own strength.
- These 300 men were instructed to surround the enemy with torches, to smash pitchers, to blow trumpets, and to shout, "A sword for the Lord and for Gideon."
- In obedience to God, the people confronted the enemy God's way, which resulted in 300 of their men routing an enemy as numerous as locusts (thousands of men).

<u>Judges 8:24-28</u>
- Despite having experienced an incredible victory, Gideon's life story did not end well.
  - ~ The fearful, doubtful one became prideful, requesting gold and wealth from the spoils of war.
  - ~ Even worse, Gideon led the people into idolatry.
- In spite of Gideon's action, God sent rest and peace to the land for forty years.

❖ **APPLICATION:** Both a reminder and a warning can be learned from Gideon's life.
  - ~ **The Reminder:** When we experience victories in our own lives, we must remember to acknowledge that it is God who gives us those victories.
  - ~ **The Warning:** Pride can often follow these "highs" in our lives.

- After Gideon Israel had eight more judges.

✝ **Judges 13:1** "Now the sons of Israel again did evil in the sight of the Lord, so that the Lord gave them into the hands of the Philistines forty years."

- After forty years of oppression by the Philistines, Israel cried out again for a deliverer.

C. Though weak in self-control <u>SAMSON</u> destroyed the Philistine rulers.

    1. God is always ready to forgive when we ask Him.

    2. Samson led Israel for <u>TWENTY</u> years.

<u>Judges 13</u>
- Samson, like John the Baptist, was dedicated to God from birth.
- His parents wanted a child but his mother was barren.
  - ~ The angel of the Lord proclaimed to them that they would have a child, a son.
- Samson was raised by godly parents, and he was blessed with great strength.

<u>Judges 16:1–25</u>
- Though physically strong, Samson was spiritually weak.
- Samson used his God-given strength for ungodly things and activities.
  - ~ He had a weakness for women and made **sinful** choices.
  - ~ He met a woman, Delilah, and she was Samson's undoing.
    - * She found the secret to his strength—it was his uncut hair.
    - * She used this knowledge against him.

⇨ **Samson lost his strength, but God would still use him in a mighty way.**

- Samson was captured by the Philistines.
  - ~ His eyes were gouged out, leaving him blind.
  - ~ He was tied between two pillars and used as an "amusement" for the enemy.

<u>Judges 16:28, 29</u>
- Samson cried out to God and his strength returned.

✝ **Judges 16:30** "And Samson said, 'Let me die with the Philistines!' And he bent with all his might so that the house fell on the lords and all the people who were in it. So the dead whom he killed at his death were more than those whom he killed in his life."

III. THE <u>CONSEQUENCES</u> OF ISRAEL'S FAILURE (JUDGES 17-21)

A. The Israelites did what was right in their <u>OWN</u> eyes.

- The final division of Judges speaks to the consequences of their failure to allow God to be their king.
- The people experienced idolatry, immorality, and civil war.
- The memory verse explains the problem: "In those days there was no king in Israel, everyone did what was right in his own eyes." (Judges 21:25)

- God was to be their king.
- Even in his prideful years, Gideon had recognized that truth. In Judges 8:23 it stated: "But Gideon said to them, 'I will not rule over you, nor shall my son rule over you; the Lord shall rule over you.'"

B. Wicked behavior shows the <u>DEPRAVITY</u> of man without God.

- When God is not king, men will always do what seems right to them, which will consistently result in wicked, sinful behavior.
- Sinful behavior demonstrates the depravity of mankind without God.
- The book of Judges ends with illustrations of what happens when God is not king.

<u>Judges 17:1-6</u>
- Because God was not the king of Israel, there was moral and religious sin leading to idolatry in the family of Micah.
  - ~ He stole silver from his mother and then used it to build a shrine to other gods.

<u>Judges 18</u>
- Because God was not the king of Israel, the priests in the tribe of Dan took Micah's idols.
- They set these idols up for the whole tribe of Dan to worship.

<u>Judges 19</u>
- Because God was not the king of Israel, a Levite allowed his concubine to be gang-raped and killed.

<u>Judges 20–21</u>
- Because God was not the king of Israel, wickedness prevailed and civil war arose among the tribes of Israel.

> **NOTE:** Did any good come from the Israelites not recognizing God as their king? We have said that choices have consequences. Doing what was "right in their own eyes" led to:
> - Stealing from one's own parent—versus honoring the parent.
> - Worshiping false idols—versus worshiping the one true God.
> - Sexual depravity—versus being holy as God had called His children to be.
> - Splintered, dysfunctional nation—versus one nation under God.

⇨ **Godliness of the previous generation does not guarantee godliness of the present one.**
  - ~ As we listen to the news today, the truth of this statement is daunting.

JUDGES
Theme: Judges Ruled

⇨ **PICTURES OF JESUS IN JUDGES**

1. Jesus is our Savior and Deliverer.

- A judge was a savior, ruler, and deliverer that God sent to rescue Israel during their darkest days.
- The judges picture Christ as our savior (or deliverer) Who rescues us from the oppressing consequences of when we do what seems right in our own eyes.
- God sent Jesus to rescue us.

2. Jesus is the King (Ruler of our lives)

- The judges also demonstrated the need that existed after one was delivered/saved—a need for a ruler.
- When we are saved by God's grace, Jesus is to become the ruler of our lives.

✛ **John 5:22–23** "For not even the Father judges anyone, but He has given all judgment to the Son, so that all will honor the Son even as they honor the Father. He who does not honor the Son does not honor the Father who sent Him."

⇨ **To live victoriously we need a righteous, holy judge to rule over us. There is only one, and His name is Jesus.**

FINAL THOUGHTS AND APPLICATION

⌷ Jesus will either be your rescuer or your judge.

> ❖ **APPLICATION:**
> ~ Have you failed God? He is listening for your cry—for true, broken-hearted repentance. There is no end to God's forgiveness.
> ~ What must we do when we have failed God through disobedience?
> * Admit your sin—confess it before God.
> * Ask for forgiveness from God.
> * Turn from what caused you to stumble in your Christian walk and move forward in obedience to Him.
> ~ Recognize that each of these actions demand a choice—an act of faith to choose what is right in God's eyes.

⌷ God must be the king of our lives or we will do what is right in our own eyes. Such an attitude will always lead to sinful actions that will negatively impact individuals, families, churches, and nations.

¤ Sadly, we often do not learn from the past but, instead, repeat it, which leads to greater defeat.

⇨ **Only when Jesus reigns as your king will you have true victory. Are you willing to turn from any cycle of sin in your life today?**

❖ <u>**FINAL APPLICATION:**</u> **Godliness of the previous generation does not guarantee godliness of the present one.**

JUDGES
Theme: Judges Ruled

JUDGES REVIEW HELPS

✧ **To the right of the column provided, write the name of the person it best describes.**

Spoke to Pharaoh

Named the animals

Killed an Egyptian

Married Rebekah

Unwanted wife with poor eyesight

Served his brother red stew

Received the Ten Commandments

Built an ark

Committed the first murder

Led the Israelites into the Promised Land

Was taken as a slave to Egypt

Chose to live in Sodom

Turned to salt

Bought Joseph in Egypt

Disagreed with the ten spies report

Took Moses' place as leader

Found a baby in the Nile

Sister who grumbled and got leprosy

Was a pillar of fire by day and cloud by night

Received land in the Promised Land

JUDGES REVIEW HELPS
(Answers for Facilitators)

✧ **To the right of the column provided, write the name of the person it best describes.**

Spoke to Pharaoh	**Aaron, Moses, or Joseph** (ONLY 1)
Named the animals	**Adam**
Killed an Egyptian	**Mose**
Married Rebekah	**Isaac**
Unwanted wife with poor eyesight	**Leah**
Served his brother red stew	**Jacob**
Received the Ten Commandments	**Moses**
Built an ark	**Noah**
Committed the first murder	**Cain**
Led the Israelites into the Promised Land	**Joshua**
Was taken as a slave to Egypt	**Joseph**
Chose to live in Sodom	**Lot**
Turned to salt	**Lot's Wife**
Bought Joseph in Egypt	**Potiphar**
Disagreed with the ten spies report	**Caleb (and Joshua)**
Took Moses' place as leader	**Joshua**
Found a baby in the Nile	**Pharaoh's Daughter**
Sister who grumbled and got leprosy	**Miriam**
Was a pillar of fire by day, cloud by night	**God**
Received land in the Promised Land	**Twelve Tribes**

RUTH

Redemption Defined

*Blessed is the LORD who has not left you
without a redeemer today.*

Ruth 4:14

SESSION EIGHT: RUTH
Redemption Defined

✝ **Memory verse:** *"Blessed is the Lord who has not left you without a redeemer today."* *(Ruth 4:14)*

- **Introduction:** The book of Ruth does not advance the history of Israel and yet it fits into the historical period during the time of the judges. It is a love story that gives a beautiful picture of redemption as Boaz redeems Ruth as her kinsman-redeemer.

- **Oral Review:** Please refer to the **REVIEW Section** in the following Teaching Guide Outline.

- **Homework:** Review the homework from the book of Judges. The following are suggestions for questions to be discussed.

    Questions on page 60
    Questions on bottom of page 63 and all of 64
    Questions at bottom of page 69 and top of page 70

- **Review Helps:** Written review is provided at the end of the teachers' presentation. (Optional and time permitting.)

- **Teacher Presentation on the Book of Ruth**

- **Learning for Life Discussion questions:** You may choose to discuss all or just one or two of the questions on page 79.

- **Closing prayer:** Pray that the students will accept Jesus Christ as their true Kinsman-Redeemer and that they will rely on Him for provision, protection, and guidance.

RUTH
Theme: Redemption Defined

TIMELINE AID FOR TEACHERS:

- **Ruth 1**   There was a famine in Bethlehem
    Elimelech moved his family to Moab
    Elimelech died
    Mahlon and Chilion married Moabite women
    Mahlon and Chilion died
    Naomi, Ruth, and Orpah began the trip back to Bethlehem
    Orpah returned to Moab, but Ruth declared her loyalty to Naomi
    Naomi and Ruth returned to Bethlehem

- **Ruth 2**   Ruth gleaned from Boaz' fields
    Boaz gave special attention to Ruth

- **Ruth 3**   Ruth uncovered Boaz' feet at the threshing floor

- **Ruth 4**   Boaz negotiated to be Elimelech's kinsman-redeemer
    Boaz and Ruth married
    Obed was born
    Obed had a son, Jesse
    Jesse had a son, David, from whom the line of Jesus came
    Boaz and Ruth came into the line of Jesus Christ

RUTH
[Redemption Defined]

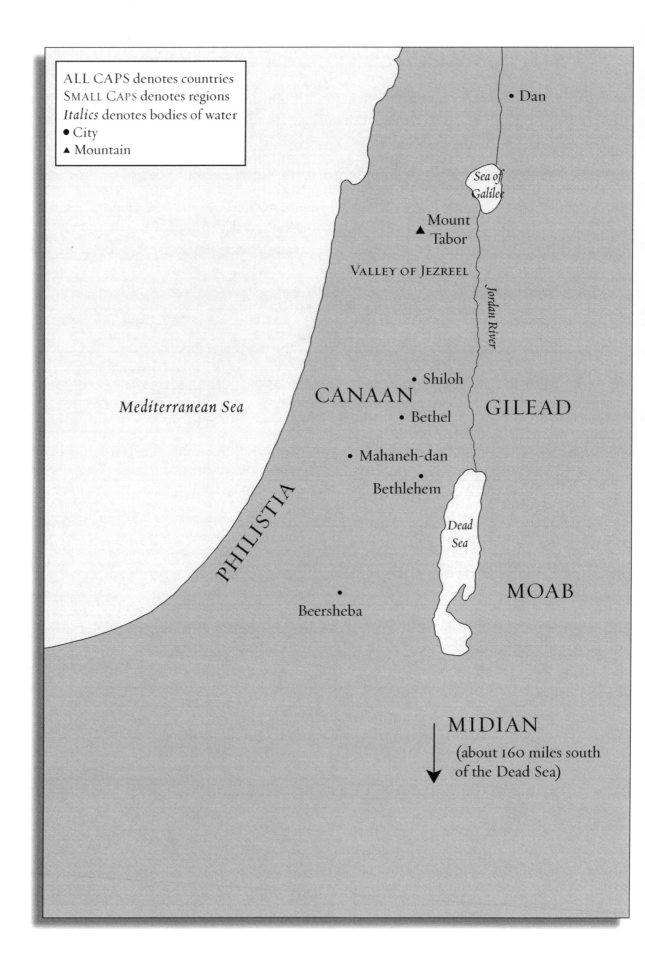

ALL CAPS denotes countries
SMALL CAPS denotes regions
Italics denotes bodies of water
● City
▲ Mountain

• Dan

Sea of Galilee

▲ Mount Tabor

VALLEY OF JEZREEL

Jordan River

• Shiloh

CANAAN

• Bethel

GILEAD

• Mahaneh-dan

Bethlehem

Mediterranean Sea

Dead Sea

PHILISTIA

MOAB

• Beersheba

MIDIAN
(about 160 miles south
of the Dead Sea)

RUTH
Theme: Redemption Defined

THE BASICS:

⇨ **Who: The Author:** Is thought to be the prophet Samuel

        Main Characters: Naomi, Ruth, Boaz

⇨ **What:** Living out the law of the kinsman-redeemer

⇨ **When:** Sometime during the time of the judges (1390–1050 B.C.). Covers about thirty years.

⇨ **Where:** The book opens in the heathen land of Moab but ends in the birthplace of redemption— Bethlehem, Israel.

⇨ **Why:** God provides redemption for all mankind.

MEMORY VERSE: *"Blessed is the Lord who has not left you without a redeemer today."*
                           Ruth 4:14

****

REVIEW:

¤ There are seventeen *historical books* in the Old Testament.

  ~ The first five or *Pentateuch* lay the foundation of God's promise of a nation with land.

  ~ The next seven, *the Kingdom books,* show the nation change from a theocracy to a monarchy.

JOSHUA

¤ This book told of Joshua leading the Israelites into the Promised Land.

¤ The people conquered the land of Canaan.

¤ Each of the twelve tribes received an allotment of land.

¤ And just as God promised—the people settled in houses that they did not build, they ate and drank from vineyards that they did not plant, and drew from wells that they did not dig. (Deuteronomy 6:10–11)

JUDGES

¤ This book continued the story from Joshua.

¤ After the death of Joshua and Eleazer (the priest), the next generations moved steadily away from God.

¤ Over the next 340 years, the Israelites fell into "cycles" of sin:

  ~ The people would <u>rebel</u>.

  ~ God would <u>reject</u> them and send enemies to oppress them.

  ~ The people would cry out to God and <u>repent</u>.

  ~ God would send a <u>rescuer</u> or a judge.

  ~ There would be <u>rest</u> as the blessings of God were restored.

RUTH
Theme: Redemption Defined

⇨ **At the end of Judges, the people had reached another morally and spiritually low period in their national history.**

OVERVIEW:

- Ruth is only one of two books in the Bible that was named after a woman.
- It is the eighth book of the Bible, and the events took place during the period of history covered in the book of Judges.
- **The Setting of Ruth:** It is one of Israel's darkest times. The nation was full of evil and bloody unrest, as the people engaged in gross immorality and ungodliness.
- **The Authorship**: Many believe that Samuel, the prophet, wrote the book of Ruth. He may have had a few reasons for penning it:
  1. It demonstrated God's faithfulness to the line of David.
  2. It provided the perfect picture of the Old Testament role of the kinsman-redeemer.
  3. It illustrated what a difference one godly woman (or man) could make, not just in a family or community, but also in a city or nation.

- Though only four chapters, Ruth is a book of light, love, and hope against the backdrop of a dark time in Israel when there was little spiritual light.

> ★ **TEACHING TIP:**
> *Have you ever considered how a jeweler presents a precious diamond? He lays it upon a dark piece of cloth, and the diamond seems to sparkle even brighter. The contrast of dark and light is obvious. The story of Ruth is the "diamond" against a dark hour in Israel's history.*

- As the story opens, Naomi, an Israelite, was living in Moab.
- After the death of her husband and two sons, Naomi decided to return to her home in Bethlehem.
- She had two daughters-in-law, Orpah and Ruth. After the death of the sons, Orpah returned to her family and Ruth remained with Naomi and traveled to Bethlehem with her.

- The book of Ruth is a beautiful story of romance; however, each of the four chapters is filled with lessons for us today.
- There are three divisions in the outline of Ruth:

  Chapter 1:   **The Heathen**—Ruth
  Chapters 2 and 3:   **The Hope**—Boaz
  Chapter 4:   **The Heir**—Obed

- In this story, Naomi and Ruth, both brokenhearted, discovered that God never forgot them. In fact, He provided a kinsman-redeemer in a man called Boaz who would rescue them and give them love, joy, safety, and security.

⇨ **The purpose of Ruth is to provide an example of a kinsman-redeemer. Jesus is our Kinsman-Redeemer.**

RUTH
Theme: Redemption Defined

I. THE HEATHEN RUTH (RUTH 1)

A. The Historical Background of Ruth

- It is helpful to have some background to the story. This is information that the Jewish reader of that time would have known.
- Naomi and her family were from Bethlehem.

1. Bethlehem means "House of <u>BREAD</u>"; yet at the time of Ruth, Bethlehem was experiencing a famine.

- If the rains did not come at the right time or if insects or disease impacted the land, then there would be a shortage of food in that area.
- Bethlehem was situated in the land of Judah, which was suffering from famine, thus food was scarce.

2. Elimelech means "My God is <u>KING</u>."

- Elimelech was Naomi's husband. He chose to leave Israel, taking Naomi and their two sons to another country.
- Though his name meant "God is my king," Elimelech's decision to move revealed that he did not truly trust God as the Almighty King Who could take care of His chosen people.
- It's possible his decision to leave Israel was that he feared God would fail him and his family.
- Naomi and Elimelech had two sons whose names were Mahlon and Chilion.

3. Mahlon means <u>WEAKLY</u> and Chilion means failing or pining.

- In the ancient east, a person's name was descriptive: it told whom they worshipped or where they were from or something about their character.
- Based on the meanings of their names, it is easy to surmise that Mahlon and Chilion were men who were physically lacking in good health or strength—being weakly, failing, and pining.
- Perhaps the description of the two sons gives insight as to why the family wanted to flee Bethlehem in the time of the famine.

- Naomi's name was also revealing.

4. Naomi, their mother, means <u>LOVELY</u> or pleasant.

- Through her name, we discover that Naomi was an attractive woman with a gentle and cheerful personality.

RUTH
Theme: Redemption Defined

- At the time she left her hometown of Bethlehem, these traits described her well but as the story unfolds that will change.

  5. **Because there was a famine, Elimelech took his family to Moab, a country that was Israel's <u>ENEMY</u>.**

- Whatever his reason for leaving Bethlehem, Elimelech knowingly chose to move into "enemy territory" for the Moabites were considered enemies of Israel.

> ★ **TEACHING TIP:**
> *If we step back and look at this scene, we see the result of not trusting God. Their self-designed plan to get food overcame any fear of the enemy and apparently any fear of disobeying God.*

REVIEW: THE MOABITES

- ¤ Introduced in Genesis. (Genesis 19:30–37)
  - ~ They were a people that began as a result of an incestuous relationship when Lot, Abraham's nephew, was seduced by his own daughter.
- ¤ Appeared again in Numbers. (Numbers 22–23)
  - ~ They refused the Israelites passage through their country when Moses was leading the Israelites through the wilderness.
  - ~ At the same time, the king of Moab also hired the prophet Balaam to curse them.
  - ~ Later, the Moabites tried to seduce the Israelites into idolatry and immorality.
- ¤ During the time of Judges, the Moabites invaded Israel and conquered her for eighteen years.
  - ~ They were cruel rulers.
  - ~ They destroyed villages and killed the people.
- ⇨ **Elimelech's decision to move his family to Moab was not a wise one.**

  B. **The Helplessness of Naomi**

  1. **Elimelech <u>DIED</u>.**

- Naomi may have thought their move to Moab would be short-lived, but a different reality set in when Elimelech died.
- As a widow, Naomi had little protection or provision from the surrounding neighbors.
  - ~ There was no one who loved the Lord to come by her side to comfort and encourage her.
  - ~ There was no friend or spiritual advisor to undergird her as she faced life alone.

2. Mahlon and Chilion married <u>MOABITE</u> women.

- Jews were not to intermarry. This was a clear command from God.

✝ **Deuteronomy 7:3** "Furthermore, you shall not intermarry with them; you shall not give your daughters to their sons, nor shall you take their daughters for your sons."

- Both sons chose to disobey God, and both married Moabite women.

> **NOTE:** Disobedience has a "ripple' effect." Here we see a father, as the spiritual leader, moving his family into "enemy" territory.
> - His act was one of distrust that led to disobedience.
> - He led his sons to live in an environment of "mingling with the enemy."
> - His lack of trust impacted his sons for we see them dismissing God's commandment on intermarrying.

- After they married, the family (including Naomi) continued to live in Moab for ten more years.

3. Mahlon and Chilion <u>DIED</u>.

- Naomi suffered another great trauma with the death of both sons, leaving her with two Moabite daughters-in-law.

Ruth 1:6–7
- Naomi learned that the famine had ended in Israel, which meant there was wheat and barley in the land to harvest.
- She decided to pack up and head back to Bethlehem; she also decided to take her daughters-in-law, Orpah and Ruth, with her.

Ruth 1:8
- Along the way Naomi stopped and told her daughters-in-law to return to their homeland, Moab, while there was still a chance for them to find other husbands to marry and have children.

> ✱ **TEACHING TIP:**
> *Naomi must have been reeling from her circumstances! Her emotions had to be running the gamut of heartache, hopelessness, confusion, and helplessness with the loss of her husband and sons. With the men gone, who would care for them?*

RUTH
Theme: Redemption Defined

> **NOTE:** What motivated Naomi to have such a change of heart and no longer think it wise for Orpah and Ruth to return to Bethlehem with her? There are several possibilities:
> - Perhaps she did not want those in Bethlehem to know her sons had married outside the faith.
> - Perhaps she was afraid for them being Moabites in Israel.
> - Perhaps she understood the challenges of being a widow in a foreign country having no citizenship, being ostracized, and removed from a community.
> - OR perhaps it was simply that Naomi loved them and did not know how she could provide and care for them.

C. Their only hope was for a KINSMAN-REDEEMER.

1. Kinsman means 'relative or kin.'
- This would be a male relative on the husband's side of the family.

2. Redeem means 'to buy back' or to 'reclaim ownership.'

3. The requirements of a kinsman redeemer were:
   a. He must be RELATED.
   b. He must be ABLE to pay the price.
   c. He must be WILLING to reclaim ownership.

- In Genesis, Leviticus, and Deuteronomy, the law of the kinsman-redeemer was carried out in two different ways:
  ~ If a man became bankrupt and had to sell his property, he could go to his rich kinsman and ask him to buy back the land for him.
    * To the Israelites, land was important; it was viewed as part of their heritage.
    * If the kinsman or relative could meet the three requirements (related, able, and willing), then he could buy back that land and give it to the man who had lost it.
    * This allowed the man and his family to stay on the land, which could then be passed down from generation to generation.
  ~ If a woman became widowed, she could go to her husband's brother or a male relative for help.
    * If the kinsman or relative was able to monetarily support her and was willing to marry her, offspring from this marriage would remain under the name of his dead brother.

* The woman would raise the child in her first husband's name, allowing the first husband's property and inheritance to go to that child and his descendants.

⇨ **A kinsman-redeemer was a male relative who was financially able and also willing to redeem.**

Ruth 1:9-13

- Based on this common practice of a kinsman-redeemer, Naomi told Orpah and Ruth that she was too old to have more sons.
  - Even if Naomi could marry quickly upon returning to Bethlehem and have sons, her daughters-in-law would not want to wait for the boys to grow into men.
  - In Naomi's frame of reference, there was no hope that either of her daughters-in-law would ever marry or have children again if they remained with her and went to Bethlehem.

> **★ TEACHING TIP:**
> *Naomi was looking into the future without considering what God could do!*

Ruth 1:9b, 15

- At first, both daughters-in-law wept and refused to leave Naomi.
- However, Orpah considered Naomi's arguments and chose to return to Moab, to her people and to her gods.
  - As the women wept, Orpah walked off the pages of history forever.

D. A flicker of <u>HOPE</u> for Naomi.

1. Ruth <u>PLEDGED</u> her heart and life to God and Naomi.

- It is here in the story that hope began.
- Hearing the same arguments, Ruth responded with some of the most poignant words ever written:

✝ **Ruth 1:16-17** "Do not urge me to leave you or turn back from following you; for where you go, I will go, and where you lodge, I will lodge. Your people shall be my people, and your God, my God. Where you die, I will die, and there I will be buried. Thus may the Lord do to me, and worse, if anything but death parts you and me."
  - Ruth made an incredible choice: to leave everything behind—her homeland, her family, her heritage, and religion.

> **★ TEACHING TIP:**
> *Ruth must have seen something special in her mother-in-law to make such a pledge of loyalty. Today these words of Ruth are often recited by a bride to her groom in wedding ceremonies. But it is quite amazing to realize that this commitment was originally spoken by a daughter-in-law to her mother-in-law!*

- She chose to entrust herself to Naomi and Naomi's God.

2. Ruth and Naomi returned to <u>BETHLEHEM.</u>

Ruth 1:18–19

- When Naomi realized that she could not convince Ruth to turn back, the two walked on to Bethlehem.

> **NOTE:** This is a great picture of God's mercy and protection.
> - Until Naomi was given an earthly redeemer, God acted as one; He protected both of the women as they returned to Bethlehem.

- Upon their arrival in Bethlehem, the villagers were stirred.
- Because of her grief, Naomi must have looked much older than the ten years that had passed.
- The people were glad to see her but were confused at first, questioning if she was Naomi.
    - ~ Her name had described her as "lovely" and "pleasant."
    - ~ Her appearance and demeanor must have contradicted those descriptions.

3. Naomi renamed herself Mara or <u>BITTER</u>.

✟ **Ruth 1:20–21** "She said to them, 'Do not call me Naomi; call me Mara, for the Almighty has dealt very bitterly with me. I went out full, but the Lord has brought me back empty. Why do you call me Naomi, since the Lord has witnessed against me and the Almighty has afflicted me?'"

- Naomi had left a famine in Israel to go to a country that was full.
- When she got to Moab, she experienced a famine of the soul.
- She left three graves in Moab and had experienced tragedy and heartache.

> ❖ **APPLICATION:** Perhaps, like Naomi, you have felt broken, helpless, and hopeless. Perhaps you have thought, "I am beyond being of any use to God. What can go wrong next? What good could possibly come from my difficulties?" We must see that Naomi had a limited and warped perspective of her circumstance for, in truth, God had been with her all the way. Consider:
> - ~ She and Ruth (two women alone) had returned to Bethlehem safely and had been protected through the long journey. (See the map in the workbook.)
> - ~ They had returned to Naomi's home in Israel—the place where widows, orphans, the poor, and aliens had a chance to make a living.

RUTH
Theme: Redemption Defined

⇨ **God had safely returned Naomi to the 'kingdom' people, a place where she could have hope.**

- It is important to consider what Ruth might have been feeling.
    - ~ She had given up everything to be with her mother-in-law who now claimed to be bitter, empty, and without hope!
- This must have been a time of anxiety and fear concerning her future but, in the second division, despair begins to have a ray of light and hope.

II. THE HOPE: BOAZ (RUTH 2–3)

Ruth 2:1
- Boaz, Elimelech's relative, is introduced as a man of great wealth.
- He fulfilled two requirements of the kinsman-redeemer:
    1. A relative of Naomi's husband, and
    2. A man of great wealth

Ruth 2:2
- Ruth needed to help provide food so, with Naomi's blessing, she went to work gleaning the barley harvest.

A. Ruth began working in Boaz's field.

Ruth 2:3
- The text states that Ruth just "happened" upon the field of Boaz.

> **★ TEACHING TIP:**
> *In God's economy, no events "just happen"! Isn't God great? Can you feel the plot thickening?*

- In those days, the gleaning process was fairly simple:
    - ~ The men usually used sickles to cut down the barley and then harvested the wheat.
    - ~ The women would come behind the men and gather and bundle the stalks, then put them on a cart.
    - ~ After this took place, those in need were permitted to glean the shafts that were left behind as God had directed in Leviticus.

✝ **Leviticus 19:9-10** "Now when you reap the harvest of your land, you shall not reap to the very corners of your field, nor shall you gather the gleanings of your harvest. Nor shall you glean your vineyard, nor shall you gather the fallen fruit of your vineyard; you shall leave them for the needy and for the stranger."

- Being a man of God, Boaz kept this law and allowed the needy to glean these fallen shafts.

Ruth 2:4-7

- While Ruth was working, Boaz came into the field and shouted to the workers, "The Lord be with you." They responded with, "May the Lord bless you."
- Boaz noticed Ruth as someone new working in his field and asked his foreman who she was.
- The foreman essentially gave these facts to Boaz:
  ~ She was a stranger (a Moabite) in the land, which meant under the law of God she was permitted to gather the gleanings of the harvest. (Leviticus 19:9–10)
  ~ She was connected to his own family through Naomi.
  ~ She was respectful because she had not gleaned until she had asked and gained permission.
  ~ She was a hard worker.

B. Boaz offered provision and protection for Ruth.

✞ **Ruth 2:8–9** "Then Boaz said to Ruth, 'Listen carefully, my daughter. Do not go to glean in another field; furthermore, do not go on from this one, but stay here with my maids. Let your eyes be on the field which they reap, and go after them. Indeed, I have commanded the servants not to touch you. When you are thirsty, go to the water jars and drink from what the servants draw.'"

- As we consider the words of Boaz to Ruth, we see that his provision and protection began here:
  ~ **His PROVISION:**
    * There was no need for her to go anywhere else to glean.
  ~ **His PROTECTION:**
    * She was told to work alongside his maidens. This would be the proper and safest company for her to keep.
    * He ordered all of his servants to be kind and respectful toward her. This would keep her safe from being ostracized or ridiculed as a foreigner.

✞ **Ruth 2:10** "Then she fell on her face, bowing to the ground and said to him, 'Why have I found favor in your sight that you should take notice of me, since I am a foreigner?'"

- Ruth's response was one of respect, humility, and gratitude.

✞ **Ruth 2:11-12** "Boaz replied to her, 'All that you have done for your mother-in-law after the death of your husband has been fully reported to me, and how you left your father and your mother and the land of your birth, and came to a people that you did not previously know. May the Lord reward your work, and your wages be full from the Lord, the God of Israel, under whose wings you have come to seek refuge.'"

- The reply of Boaz spoke to the goodness of Ruth's character that had made an impression on the people of Bethlehem.

> **NOTE:** Boaz understood the difficulty of being a foreign woman in a foreign land.
> - That was his mother, Rahab's story.
> - In the book of Joshua we met Rahab, the harlot. She lived in Jericho, and it was in her home that the two Israelite spies were hidden and protected.
> - At that time, she also expressed her belief in their God.
> - When the city of Jericho was taken by the Israelites, Rahab and her family were spared as promised by the spies.
> - She married Salmon, an Israelite, and gave birth to a son, Boaz. Rahab's name would ultimately be in the genealogy of Jesus Christ! (Matthew 1:5)
>
> ⇨ **Perhaps Boaz was treating Ruth as he had witnessed others treat his own mother. In effect, he was embracing her into the family of God.**

Ruth 2:14-18

- Later that same day, Boaz invited Ruth to share a meal of bread and vinegar with the reapers and he personally served her roasted grain.
- After the meal was over and Ruth had left the table to return to the field, Boaz gave instructions to his field hands regarding her:
  ~ They were not to insult or harass her as she gleaned in his field; they were to treat her kindly.
  ~ They were to leave extra grain on the ground so she could gather an abundance of grain.
- Thus, that same day Ruth gathered barley, beat out the kernels, and returned to Naomi with enough grain to feed them both for five days.

Ruth 2:19–23

- Naomi asked, "Where did you glean today and where did you work?"
- Ruth shared with her mother-in-law that she had been working in the field of Boaz.
- Naomi responded with words of a blessing for Boaz and praise to God: "May he be blessed of the Lord who has not withdrawn his kindness to the living and to the dead." (Ruth 2:20)

- Naomi also revealed to Ruth that Boaz was one of her husband's closest relatives, and she told Ruth to stay in his field and work alongside his maids.

✝ **Ruth 3:1** "Then Naomi her mother-in-law said to her, 'My daughter, shall I not seek security for you, that it may be well with you?'"

- Naomi expressed her concern for Ruth—the idea behind the word "security" in this verse was marriage. Even though Naomi seemed not to want to remarry, she did not want Ruth, as a young woman, to be confined to widowhood.
- Naomi also thought that Boaz was very well the closest living relative, thus would be the one who could "redeem" Ruth and have her become his wife.

- Naomi instructed Ruth to do something that might secure Ruth's future.

✝ **Ruth 3:3-5** "'Wash yourself therefore, and anoint yourself and put on your best clothes, and go down to the threshing floor; but do not make yourself known to the man until he has finished eating and drinking. It shall be when he lies down, that you shall notice the place where he lies, and you shall go and uncover his feet and lie down; then he will tell you what you shall do.' She said to her, 'All that you say I will do.'"

> **NOTE:** It is very hard not to ask the questions, "What kind of instructions were these? Why in the world would Naomi suggest such a plan to Ruth?" We cannot give a solid answer to these questions; we can only consider the situation in light of that culture at that time:
> - Naomi believed that Boaz was their closest living relative in regards to Elimelech and Mahlon. In her mind this meant that Boaz, under the law, could be their potential kinsman-redeemer.
> - Naomi appeared to want Ruth to be the one to remind Boaz of this relationship because they had developed an acquaintance.
> - Naomi did NOT instruct Ruth to appear as a harlot. There was no immorality suggested in her actions or appearance.
> - Naomi also did NOT instruct Ruth to lie at Boaz' side, which may have compromised her; instead she instructed Ruth to lie at his feet.
> - Naomi also knew the character of Boaz: he was a godly man with integrity and could be trusted when Ruth appeared, laying at his feet.
> - Naomi's instructions to Ruth can seem a bit confusing, but the story clearly shows that both Ruth and Boaz were people of great character. It is clear that Boaz was the man that Naomi believed him to be for he did not violate Ruth.

RUTH
Theme: Redemption Defined

Ruth 3: 6–11

- Ruth did exactly as Naomi had instructed.
- She went to the threshing floor and did not show herself to Boaz while there.
- After Boaz had eaten, he retired and lay down by the grain to protect it through the night. Ruth secretly entered the room, uncovered his feet, and laid down there.
- Boaz woke with a surprise and asked, "Who are you?"
- Ruth's responded, "I am Ruth your maid. So spread your covering over your maid, for you are a close relative." (Ruth 3:9)
  - ~ This was an important step because, in effect, Ruth was giving Boaz permission to pursue her as a kinsman-redeemer.
- Boaz was flattered and honored and spread his covering (blanket/mantle) over her.

> **★ TEACHING TIP:**
> *To "spread a skirt over another" is, in the East, a symbolic action signifying protection. Even to the present day, when a Jew marries a woman, he throws the skirt or end of his talith (Hebrew cloak or mantle) over her, to signify that he has taken her under his protection.*

REVIEW:

- ⌘ We have seen this expression of "spread your covering" earlier in Ruth in the story.
- ✝ **Ruth 2:12** "May the Lord reward your work, and your wages be full from the Lord, the God of Israel, under whose wings you have come to seek refuge."

- Boaz referenced the refuge of God's wings in his blessing for her as she worked in the field to provide for Naomi.

Ruth 3:12–13

- Boaz, being a man of integrity, told Ruth that he actually was not the closest relative to Elimelech and Mahlon.
- He promised to go seek out the closest relative and ask if he would be her kinsman-redeemer. If this relative declined, then Boaz would become her kinsman-redeemer.
  - ~ With this promise, Boaz was ensuring that Elimelech's land would be bought back.
  - ~ Elimelech and Mahlon would have an heir and a benefactor to whom their name would be passed.
- Boaz had Ruth stay the night and leave early the next morning for two reasons:
  1. Her safety—it would not be safe for a woman to travel alone at night.
  2. Her reputation—he wanted to ensure that her reputation would not be tarnished by anyone seeing her leave the room and presume the worst.

- Boaz sent her home with eighty pounds of grain so that she would not return to Naomi empty-handed.
- And, Naomi told Ruth to "rest and wait," and she did.

C. Boaz became Ruth's <u>KINSMAN REDEEMER</u>.
 1. He was <u>RELATED.</u>
 2. He was <u>ABLE.</u>
 3. He was <u>WILLING.</u>

<u>Ruth 4:1–12</u>

- Boaz went to the city gate, which was the place where business in the city was transacted.
- A close relative of Elimelech passed by, and Boaz stopped and asked him to sit down. He then invited ten elders to meet with them.
- Boaz proposed that the relative redeem the land Elimelech had owned. The relative agreed at first, until he was told that this would also involve taking Ruth as his wife.
- Even though he was a relative and was able to be a kinsman-redeemer, the relative was unwilling to redeem the land because marriage to Ruth would jeopardize his own inheritance.
- The relative handed Boaz his sandal, and Boaz accepted it.

> ⇨ **Boaz accepted the role of kinsman-redeemer.**

> ★ **TEACHING TIP:**
> *What an incredible instruction to a young woman who had lost her husband, left everything familiar behind her, and had worked tirelessly gleaning in the field to support her mother-in-law and herself.*

> ★ **TEACHING TIP:**
> *Though a seemingly odd action, this gesture with the sandal would be similar to what we do today by "shaking hands" on an agreement.*

D. Boaz and Ruth married.
- Boaz took Ruth as his wife, and God gave her hope. (Ruth 4:13)
- The remainder of the book of Ruth reveals where the line of David began.

III.   THE HEIR: OBED (RUTH 4)

A. Obed was Ruth's son and his name means 'servant.'

<u>Ruth 4:13–22</u>

- Boaz and Ruth give birth to Obed.
- At his birth, the neighbor women gave testimony to the blessings of God upon Naomi.
  - ~ God had not left her without a redeemer.

> ~ God had provided her with a daughter-in-law who loved her in an exceptional manner.
> ~ God had provided care and protection for Naomi for the rest of her life.

- It is interesting to note that these neighbor women were the ones who named the baby Obed.

B. Obed's son was <u>JESSE.</u>

- The name Jesse means "gift, God's gift."

C. Jesse was the father of <u>DAVID</u>, who became the King of Israel.

- David means "beloved."
- David was Jesse's youngest son.
- He became the second and greatest king that Israel ever had.
  - ~ He united the nation.
  - ~ He brought the people back to God.
  - ~ He established Jerusalem as the capital and center of worship.
  - ~ He brought peace and security to the people.
- Under David's leadership, Israel was established as a strong and powerful nation.
- He was a man after God's own heart.

D. David was in the line of <u>JESUS CHRIST</u>, the King of kings and the Lord of lords.

- David had descendants, with the most famous child being Jesus Christ.

⇨ <u>PICTURES OF JESUS IN RUTH (E in workbook)</u>

E. Jesus is our <u>KINSMAN REDEEMER</u>

1. He is <u>RELATED</u>. (He became a man)

2. He was <u>ABLE</u>. (To pay the price for our sins)

3. He was <u>WILLING</u>. (unto death)

RUTH
Theme: Redemption Defined

FINAL THOUGHTS AND APPLICATION

⌘ Ruth is a story of a family versus a nation (as in Judges).

⌘ It takes place during the days of the judges yet stands in stark contrast to the book of Judges!

   ~ Instead of violence and lawlessness, we are told a story of love, tenderness, and sacrifice.

⌘ In this love story, there were several sub-plots:

   1. One spoke of the loyal love between a mother-in-law and a daughter-in-law.
   2. One illustrated the protective, caring love of a Kinsman-Redeemer, as seen in the relationship between Boaz and Ruth.
   3. And the Lord's faithful, ever-present love worked through these human relationships.

⌘ This book reminds us of the providence of God and His redemptive plan. God is at work:

   ~ No matter how dire the circumstances may be.
   ~ No matter how hopeless and broken we may "feel."
   ~ His desire is to redeem you.

⇨ **Jesus is the only Kinsman-Redeemer: related, able, and willing to redeem <u>you</u>. Is He yours?**

❖ **FINAL APPLICATION: We all have a need of, and hope for, a Redeemer.**

RUTH REVIEW HELPS

✧ **Match the Theme with the Book of The Bible**

Theme	**Book of the Bible**
Land conquered	Genesis
Book of unbelief	Exodus
Book of beginnings	Leviticus
Book of deliverance	Numbers
Book of obedience	Deuteronomy
Book of holiness	Joshua
The judges ruled	Judges
Redemption defined	Ruth
The Sin Cycle	
God the deliverer	
God the creator	
The land settled	
Blessings and curses	
Offerings and Feasts	
Wilderness wandering	

- **The five Pentateuch Books are:**   **There are _____ books in the Bible**

1.

2.

3.

4.

5.

RUTH REVIEW HELPS

✧ **Choose from the list at the bottom of the page the word(s) that best fits with God's actions.**

God created the heavens and the earth, man and woman: _____

God saved the only righteous and his family: _____

God promised he would become a great nation: _____

God took him from a pit to the palace: _____

God brought her a baby in a basket: _____

God trained him in a royal family and then as a shepherd: _____

God chose him to help his brother lead the people to freedom: _____

God used ten of these to discipline Egypt: _____

God gave the people these laws for excellent living: _____

God gave the people a tent to remind them that God was with them _____

God rewarded the two spies who trusted in Him _____ _____

God provided for their every need even in discipline_____

God gave them sermons to remind them of the past, present, and future: _____

God told him to "fear not" and then gave him the land: _____

God made the great wall fall: _____

God called him a mighty warrior even though he was afraid: _____

God chose a woman to lead and judge Israel: _____

God gave him unusual strength: _____

Adam and Eve	Moses	Joseph
Pharaoh's daughter	Ten Commandments	Plagues
Tabernacle	Jericho	Joshua
Deuteronomy	Noah	Gideon
Deborah	Samson	Abraham
Aaron	Wandering	Caleb

RUTH REVIEW HELPS
(Answers for Facilitators)

◇ **Match the Theme with the Book of The Bible**

Theme	**Book of the Bible**
Land conquered	**Joshua**
Book of unbelief	**Numbers**
Book of beginnings	**Genesis**
Book of deliverance	**Exodus**
Book of obedience	**Deuteronomy**
Book of holiness	**Leviticus**
The judges ruled	**Judges**
Redemption defined	**Ruth**
The Sin Cycle	**Judges**
God the deliverer	**Exodus**
God the creator	**Genesis**
The land settled	**Joshua**
Blessings and Curses	**Deuteronomy**
Offerings and Feasts	**Leviticus**
Wilderness wandering	**Numbers**

The five Pentateuch Books are:
1. **Genesis**
2. **Exodus**
3. **Leviticus**
4. **Numbers**
5. **Deuteronomy**

There are **66** books in the Bible.

RUTH REVIEW HELPS
(Answers for Facilitators)

✧ **Choose from the list at the bottom of the page the word(s) that best fits with God's actions.**

God created the heavens and the earth, man and woman: **Adam and Eve**

God saved the only righteous and his family: **Noah**

God promised he would become a great nation: **Abraham**

God took him from a pit to the palace: **Joseph**

God brought her a baby in a basket: **Pharaoh's daughter**

God trained him in a royal family and then as a shepherd: **Moses**

God chose him to help his brother lead the people to freedom: **Aaron**

God used ten of these to discipline Egypt: **plagues**

God gave the people these laws for excellent living: **Ten commandments**

God gave the people a tent to remind them that God was with them: **Tabernacle**

God rewarded the two spies who trusted in Him: **Joshua, Caleb**

God provided for their every need even in discipline: **Wandering**

God gave them sermons to remind them of the past, present and future: **Deuteronomy**

God told him to "fear not" and then gave him the land: **Joshua**

God made the great wall fall: **Jericho**

God called him a mighty warrior even though he was afraid: **Gideon**

God chose a woman to lead and judge Israel: **Deborah**

God gave him unusual strength: **Samson**

Adam and Eve	Moses	Joseph
Pharaoh's daughter	Ten Commandments	Plagues
Tabernacle	Jericho	Joshua
Deuteronomy	Noah	Gideon
Deborah	Samson	Abraham
Aaron	Wandering	Caleb

FIRST SAMUEL

The Monarchy Established

Man looks at the outward appearance,
but the LORD looks at the heart.

1 Samuel 16:7

SESSION NINE: FIRST SAMUEL
The Monarchy Established

✝ **Memory Verse:** *"... man looks at the outward appearance, but the Lord looks at the heart." (1 Samuel 16:7b)*

- **Introduction:** First Samuel continues the history of Israel from the book of Judges. After continually failing to live in obedience to God, the people demanded a king like all the other nations so he would lead them into battle. Samuel, the last judge, warned the people they would not be happy with a human king but they insisted, so Saul became the first king of Israel and the monarchy was established.

- **Oral Review:** Please refer to the **REVIEW Section** in the following Teaching Guide Outline.

- **Homework**: Review the homework for the book of Ruth. The following are key questions to be discussed.

    Questions at the bottom of page 84
    All questions on page 87
    All questions on page 90
    Question in the middle of page 93

- **Review Helps:** Written review is provided at the end of the teachers' presentation. (Optional and time permitting.)

- **Teacher Presentation on the Book of 1 Samuel**

- **Learning for Life Discussion questions:** You may choose to discuss all or just one or two of the questions on page 103.

- **Closing prayer**: End with prayer asking God to strengthen each heart so that God would remain on the throne of their lives as the Eternal and Sovereign King as they submit to His will for their lives.

FIRST SAMUEL
Theme: The Monarchy Established

TIMELINE AID FOR TEACHERS:

- **1 Samuel 1 –8   The Life of Samuel**
  - ~ Samuel was born a judge, priest, and prophet
  - ~ Under Samuel's leadership, the Philistines were defeated and the ark returned to Israel
  - ~ Israel rejected Samuel's sons as leaders and God as their king; they demanded a human king

- **1 Samuel 9–15   The Reign of Saul**
  - ~ Saul became king and had early success fighting against the Ammonites
  - ~ Saul failed by:
    (1) Presumptuously acting as a priest
    (2) Disobeying God by not utterly defeating Amalek and lying about it
    (3) Seeking a medium instead of God
  - ~ God rejected Saul as king

- **1 Samuel 16–31 The Faithfulness of David, God's Chosen King**
  - ~ David was anointed to be king
  - ~ David defeated Goliath
  - ~ David and Jonathan, Saul's son, had a covenant relationship
  - ~ Saul attempted many times to kill David, but Jonathan would warn David
  - ~ David ran for his life, hiding in the wilderness
  - ~ Saul committed suicide during battle

I Samuel
[Monarchy Established]

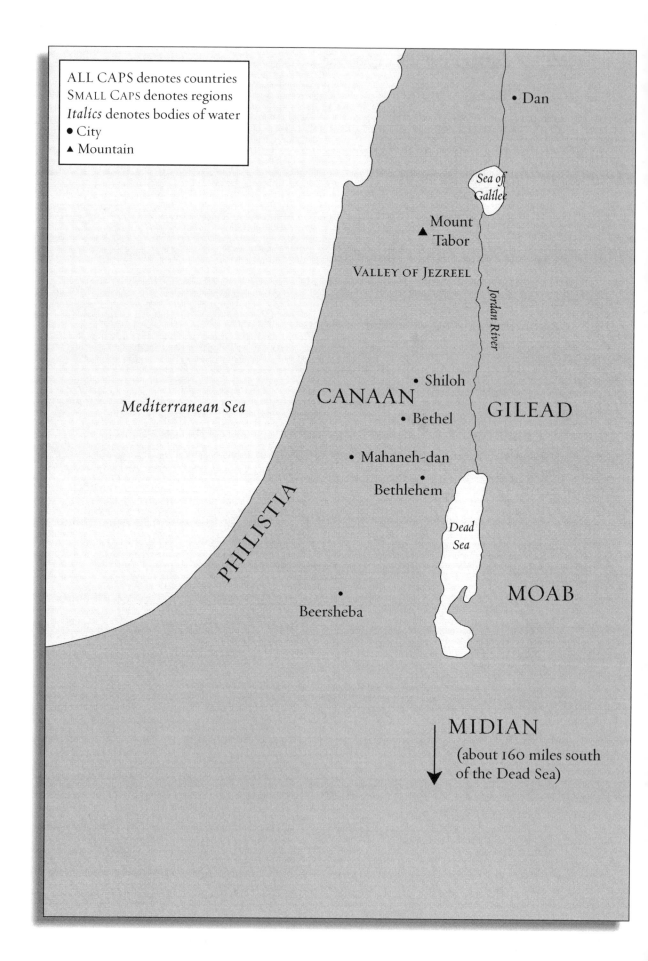

ALL CAPS denotes countries
SMALL CAPS denotes regions
Italics denotes bodies of water
• City
▲ Mountain

• Dan

Sea of Galilee

▲ Mount Tabor

VALLEY OF JEZREEL

Jordan River

Mediterranean Sea

CANAAN

• Shiloh

• Bethel

GILEAD

• Mahaneh-dan

• Bethlehem

Dead Sea

PHILISTIA

MOAB

• Beersheba

MIDIAN

(about 160 miles south of the Dead Sea)

FIRST SAMUEL
Theme: The Monarchy Established

THE BASICS:

⇨ **Who:** **The Author:** Believed to have been written by Samuel with additions written by the prophets, Gad and Nathan

   The Main Characters: Samuel, Saul, David

⇨ **What:** "Give us a king!" Israel becomes a monarchy

⇨ **When:** Covers ninety-four years—from the birth of Samuel, the last judge (1105 B.C.), to the death of Saul, the first king (1011 B.C.)

⇨ **Where:** Canaan (Israel)

⇨ **Why:** Israel's theocracy becomes a monarchy when the people demand a king.

MEMORY VERSE: *"... man looks at the outward appearance, but the Lord looks at the heart."*
1 Samuel 16:7b

****

REVIEW:

THE PENTATEUCH

⌖ The Pentateuch is comprised of five books:

~ **Genesis:** The book of beginnings—Creation, the human race, the fall of man, and the chosen race. God made a covenant with Abraham that held three promises: a nation, a land, and, eventually, a descendant who would bless the world.

~ **Exodus:** The book of deliverance—under the leadership of Moses, the Israelites were delivered from bondage in Egypt. The Ten Commandments were given, and the tabernacle was constructed according to the instructions given by God.

~ **Leviticus:** The book of holiness—God gave additional laws for holy worship and holy living.

~ **Numbers:** The book of unbelief—the Israelites came to the edge of the Promised Land, but unbelief and fear caused the people to refuse to take on the conquest of Canaan. This generation wandered for forty years in the wilderness until they all died.

~ **Deuteronomy:** The book of obedience—God gave the next generation a second chance. He prepared them to enter the land by repeating the laws to govern their society and their relationship with Him.

⇨ **These books presented man's need for a Savior and God's redemptive plan.**

THE KINGDOM BOOKS

⌖ These books continue the story of the Israelites. Through them we learn how the theocratic nation of Israel became a monarchy or kingdom.

FIRST SAMUEL
Theme: The Monarchy Established

JOSHUA
¤ Canaan was conquered by Joshua and divided into twelve independent territories for the tribes descended from Jacob's sons.

¤ Once the people were in the land, they told Joshua, "We will serve the Lord our God and we will obey His voice." (Joshua 24:24)

JUDGES
¤ The people did not obey God for long because: "In those days there was no king in Israel; everyone did what was right in his own eyes." (Judges 21:25)

¤ This led to seven sin cycles: The people would _**rebel**_ > God would **reject** them and send an enemy nation to oppress them > the people would cry out to the Lord and **repent** > God would send a **rescuer** or a judge to deliver them > there would be **rest** > then this cycle would repeat itself.

¤ Oftentimes when a judge died, the people would go back through the sin cycle again.

¤ This was a dark time in the nation's history with immorality, idolatry, and civil war.

RUTH
¤ This is a story of light and hope in the same dark time period as Judges.

¤ It gives an example of the qualifications and role of a kinsman-redeemer in the man Boaz who redeemed Ruth.

¤ It is a picture of the Redeemer to come.

OVERVIEW:

▪ In the original Hebrew, 1 and 2 Samuel were written as one book.

▪ First Samuel covers ninety-four years beginning with the birth of Samuel, who was the last judge, and ending with the death of Saul, the first king.

▪ Some of the time period in the book of Judges overlaps with the book of 1 Samuel.

▪ Therefore, it was written at a time when Israel, the nation, was morally corrupt and militarily weak.

▪ Israel was in a period of transition—from being a nation of twelve loosely connected tribes led by local leaders to becoming a united nation under one king.

▪ Under the twelve-tribe system, there was often more than one judge serving at a time.
~ A good example of this would be Samuel and Samson who were both judges and also contemporaries.

⇨ **The purpose of 1 Samuel is to show the consequences when people demand a human king to replace God, their King.**

▪ The rule of the judges came to an end in 1 Samuel, and the rule of the kings began.

▪ Israel was formed as a theocracy—God was to be their king.

FIRST SAMUEL
Theme: The Monarchy Established

- However, the people wanted and demanded to have a man as their king.
- If you are one who enjoys biographies, then you will like this book as it delves into the story of three men: Samuel, Saul, and David.
- The story of Samuel begins with his mother, Hannah.

I. THE LIFE OF SAMUEL (1 SAMUEL 1–8)

A. Hannah trusted God and He gave her a son, Samuel.

- Hannah was a woman with problems: in her country, in her family, and in her religious community.
- The problem in the country was due to the fact that "everyone was doing what was right in their own eyes." Such problems in a country will often impact believing families.

1 Samuel 1:2-8

- The culture of that time directly impacted Hannah's family. Her husband, Elkanah, had two wives, Hannah and Peninnah.
  - ~ Having two wives was not in God's will. He had created one woman, Eve, for Adam.
- Hannah had two problems with this family arrangement:
  1. Peninnah had given birth to sons and daughters while Hannah was unable to conceive.
  2. Peninnah also provoked Hannah bitterly. It is very likely this needling was about Hannah's barrenness. Whatever the subject, it caused Hannah to weep and made her unable to eat.

- In her great anguish over her inability to conceive, Hannah went to the temple to pray to God and there she also made a vow:

✝ **1 Samuel 1:10–11** "She, greatly distressed, prayed to the Lord and wept bitterly. She made a vow and said, 'O Lord of hosts, if You will indeed look on the affliction of Your maidservant and remember me, and not forget Your maidservant, but will give Your maidservant a son, then I will give him to the Lord all the days of his life, and a razor shall never come on his head.'"

- Hannah prayed earnestly, moving her lips, yet making no sound.

1 Samuel 1:12-20

- Eli, the priest, saw Hannah and thought she was drunk!
- When he realized that she was praying he said to her, "Go in peace; and may the God of Israel grant your petition that you have asked of Him." (1 Samuel 1:17)

- Hannah returned home. She ate and was no longer sad, because she trusted God and experienced joy.
- Hannah did have a baby, and she named him Samuel, which means "asked of God" or "God heard."

B. Eli, the unfaithful priest, raised Samuel from the time he was weaned.

- Hannah had a son, but she had made a vow: If God gave her a baby, she would give him back to God.
- She kept her vow.

> **NOTE:** The Bible speaks to the importance of honoring one's vows. It is a simple instruction—if you make a vow, keep it! Hannah is a great example of this.
> ✝ **Deuteronomy 23:21** "When you make a vow to the Lord your God, you shall not delay to pay it, for it would be sin in you, and the Lord your God will surely require it of you."
> ✝ **Ecclesiastes 5:4–5** "When you make a vow to God, do not be late in paying it; for He takes no delight in fools. Pay what you vow! It is better that you should not vow than that you should vow and not pay."

1 Samuel 2:1–20

- Samuel was only three to five years old when Hannah took him to Eli, the priest.
- This was a huge act of faith on Hannah's part because Eli's parenting skills were lacking: "Now the sons of Eli were worthless men; they did not know the Lord…" (1 Samuel 2:12)
- What a sad verse! To make matters worse, Eli's sons were priests: "Thus the sin of the young men was very great before the Lord, for the men despised the offering of the Lord." (1 Samuel 2:17)

> ★ **TEACHING TIP:**
> *We said earlier that there were problems in the religious community. The sons of Eli help us better understand the scene. Here we have two men acting as priests who did not know the Lord, and they broke God's religious laws.*

1 Samuel 2:22–29

- The sons also broke God's moral laws:

✝ **1 Samuel 2:22** "Now Eli was very old; and he heard all that his sons were doing to all Israel, and how they lay with the women who served at the doorway of the tent of meeting."

- They were having intimate relationships with the women serving God!
- God chastised Eli saying, "… you … honor your sons above Me, by making yourselves fat with the choicest of every offering of my people Israel." (1 Samuel 2:29)
    ~ The sons, as priests, were stealing the sacrifices that the people were bringing to God.
    ~ They were taking money out of the offering plate and putting it in their own pocket.

> ★ **TEACHING TIP:**
>
> *How tragic! Can you imagine being Hannah and taking your child to live with a father such as Eli? It would have been very easy for Hannah to justify and rationalize not keeping the vow she had made to God. Leaving Samuel with Eli was a real act of faith.*

1 Samuel 2:29–34

- God spoke to Eli regarding his sons. Because Eli had honored his sons above God, his sons were going to die.

1 Samuel 3:1–14

- Young Samuel was in the house of the Lord ministering before Eli.
- A word from the Lord was rare in those days and visions were infrequent.
- Samuel awoke one night and heard a voice calling his name.
- He ran immediately to Eli and said, "Here I am, for you called me." But Eli responded, "I did not call, lie down again." (1 Samuel 3:5)
- Three times this occurred when Eli finally discerned that it was God calling Samuel.
- Eli told Samuel to lie down and, if God called to him, say, "Speak, Lord, for your servant is listening." (1 Samuel 3:9b)
- Samuel obeyed and God did speak.

✟ **1 Samuel 3:11–14** "The Lord said to Samuel, 'Behold, I am about to do a thing in Israel at which both ears of everyone who hears it will tingle. In that day I will carry out against Eli all that I have spoken concerning his house, from beginning to end. For I have told him that I am about to judge his house forever for the iniquity which he knew, because his sons brought a curse on themselves and he did not rebuke them. Therefore I have sworn to the house of Eli that the iniquity of Eli's house shall not be atoned for by sacrifice or offering forever.'"

- In Deuteronomy, God had said that there would be blessings for obedience and curses for disobedience.
- Eli's sons were obviously disobeying God; and Eli did not love them enough to do something about their disobedience. He did not discipline or rebuke them regarding their sinful behavior.

❖ **APPLICATION:** The story of Eli and his sons should speak to all parents.
~ If, as a father or mother, we see our children disobeying God's Word, then we are called by God to discipline them and to help them.
~ We are not to be like Eli who apparently stood by and did nothing, even though he was fully aware of their disobedience.

C. **Samuel's offices included:**

1. **He was Israel's last and most effective <u>JUDGE</u>.**

2. **He was Israel's first <u>PROPHET</u>.**

3. **He served as a <u>PRIEST</u>.**

D. **He was chosen by God for these offices.**

▪ He was chosen by God, called by God, and he always sought God.

▪ The people and priests, however, were not seeking God.

<u>1 Samuel 4</u>

▪ The priests <u>rebelled</u> against God, so God <u>rejected</u> them and sent the Philistines who defeated Israel.

▪ After the defeat, the priests said, "Let us take to ourselves from Shiloh the ark of the covenant of the Lord, that it may come among us and deliver us from the power of our enemies." (1 Samuel 4:3b)

~ The ark was a visible symbol of God's presence.

~ The implication here was that, if they took the ark, God's presence would be with them.

~ It is important to note that the priests did not address their own rebellion (sin).

<u>REVIEW</u>—The History of the Ark of the Covenant

⌑ The ark of the covenant was placed in the Holy of Holies in the tabernacle.

⌑ God Himself dwelt in the Holy of Holies and **only** the High Priest was permitted to enter it once a year and only on the Day of Atonement when he would offer a blood sacrifice to "cover" the sins of the people.

⌑ In fact, tradition tells us that the high priest would put a rope around his waist so that he could be pulled out in case God struck him dead!

- Eli's sons knew this yet, in total disobedience, they went into the tabernacle and brought the ark of God back from Shiloh.
  ~ It was not the Day of Atonement.
  ~ Neither son was the high priest.
  ~ Yet they went in and brought out the ark of God, so that "it" could help them fight their enemies.

- It is no surprise that Israel lost the next battle.
- And the two sons of Eli were killed just as God had said.
- In addition, the Philistines took the ark of God back to Philistine territory.
- When Eli learned that his sons had died, that Israel had been defeated, and that the ark had been taken, he fell over backwards and died.
- During this time, one of Eli's daughters-in-law went into labor and had a son whom she called Ichabod which means "the glory has departed from Israel."

1 Samuel 5
- The Philistines took the ark into the temple of their god, Dagon, who was the father of Baal.
- The next morning, they found their god lying flat on his face!
- They set him upright. However, the following morning their idol was not only on his face again, but his hands and neck had been cut off.

⇨ **It was as if God was saying that any gods that men created for themselves would fall on their face in the presence of Almighty God.**

- The Philistines were afraid so they sent the Ark of the Covenant to Gath; the men there broke out in tumors!
- So the ark was sent to Ekron. The people there said:
✝ **1 Samuel 5:10b–11a** "... They have brought the ark of the God of Israel around to us, to kill us and our people ... Send away the ark of the God of Israel, and let it return to its own place ..."

- The people of Ekron wanted to be rid of the ark so they gathered all the lords of the Philistines to determine what to do with it. Scripture states that "... there was deadly confusion throughout the city; the hand of God was very heavy there." (1 Samuel 5:11b)

1 Samuel 6
- The ark had been in the country of the Philistines for seven months when the priests and diviners were called in to determine what they should do with the ark.

- These "consultants" stated that they should send the ark back to Israel—but they also advised that a "guilt offering" be sent with the ark. This offering was comprised of five golden tumors and five golden mice.

> **NOTE:** Why five golden tumors and five golden mice?
> - The number five represented the number of Philistine lords.
> - The tumors and mice represented the malady and infestation that had afflicted the Philistines.
> - Gold represented the most precious metal. Using this metal emphasized the idea of how willing they were to purchase their peace with the God of Israel.

- The people did as they were advised and sent the ark on its way.

✠ **1 Samuel 6:9** "Watch, if it goes up by the way of its own territory to Beth-shemesh, then He has done us this great evil. But if not, then we will know that it was not His hand that struck us; it happened to us by chance."
  - ~ The Philistines believed that if the cart headed back to Canaan, then it confirmed that the God of Israel had afflicted them, indeed. If the cart headed in another direction, then their maladies had simply happened by chance.
- The cart headed straight to Israel!
- The Israelites were reaping their wheat in the valley when they saw the cart.
- The people were elated because God's glory had returned to Israel.

1 Samuel 6:13–21
- The people killed the cows that had also accompanied the ark and made a sacrifice.
- They also made a critically bad decision; they opened the lid of the ark and looked inside of it!
  - ~ God had made it clear that man could not look at holy objects. (Numbers 4:20)
  - ~ God was true to His Word for over 50,000 people died that day in Israel because of their disobedience.

⇨ **What a contrast between faithful Hannah and faithful Samuel with the unfaithful priests and people.**
  - ~ We live in a similar world because, when every man does what is right in his own eyes, the result will be unfaithfulness.

1 Samuel 8
- Samuel was an old man when he appointed his sons as judges over Israel.

- Sadly, there was a problem with his sons: "His sons, however, did not walk in his ways, but turned aside after dishonest gain and took bribes and perverted justice." (1 Samuel 8:3)

> **NOTE:** Samuel's mother had been a godly mother with a godly and faithful son, Samuel. Why were Samuel's sons unfaithful? There are a few things to be considered:
> - Eli had been Samuel's example of a father, yet he was not a good one.
> - This may be an example of how strong society's pull can be on a godly family.
> - Because Samuel was a judge who had to travel from city to city, year after year, it may be that he was an absentee father who was not around to discipline his sons. (See 1 Samuel 7:15–17)
> - Or, perhaps, this is simply a good illustration that none of us get to God on the "family plan." Each of us has to make a personal decision regarding Who God is and Who He is to us.

- We do not know why Samuel's sons were not faithful, but we do know that their unfaithfulness had a great impact on the people.

✞ **1 Samuel 8:5–6** "'Behold, you have grown old, and your sons do not walk in your ways. Now appoint a king for us to judge us like all the nations.' But the thing was displeasing in the sight of Samuel when they said, 'Give us a king to judge us.'"

E. He sought God's guidance through prayer all his life.

- The people did not want Samuel's sons to lead them. Instead, they wanted a king as their judge.
- Samuel did not receive this request well so he went to the Lord in prayer, and the Lord answered him.

✞ **1 Samuel 8:7–9** "The Lord said to Samuel, 'Listen to the voice of the people in regard to all that they say to you, for they have not rejected you, but they have rejected Me from being king over them. Like all the deeds which they have done since the day that I brought them up from Egypt even to this day—in that they have forsaken Me and served other gods—so they are doing to you also. Now then, listen to their voice; however, you shall solemnly warn them and tell them of the procedure of the king who will reign over them.'"

FIRST SAMUEL
Theme: The Monarchy Established

> **NOTE:** The people wanted a king—how foolish!
> - God was their king.
> - It was God who had led them through the wilderness, provided the manna, and protected them.
> - They had the best king they could have, but they wanted to be like all the other nations that had human kings. (See 1 Samuel 8:5) How sad!
> - They were not to be like everybody else. God had chosen them to be different as His chosen people.

- **God's perspective:** The people's demand for a king was essentially an act of rejecting Him.

- **God's instruction to Samuel:** Warn the people about what they were requesting.

<u>1 Samuel 8:10–17</u>
- **Samuel's warning:** If the people had a king he would:
  1. Take their sons for military service.
  2. Take their daughters to be perfumers, cooks, and bakers.
  3. Take the best of their fields, vineyards, and olive groves.
  4. Tax them—take 1/10 of their seed, vineyards, and flocks.
  5. Take their servants, best young men, and donkeys to use them for his work.
  6. Make the people his servants.

⇨ **God warned the people that having a human king would cost them dearly.**

- **People's response**: They refused to listen to Samuel's warning. They wanted a "human" king!

✝ **1 Samuel 8:19–20** "Nevertheless, the people refused to listen to the voice of Samuel, and they said, 'No, but there shall be a king over us, that we also may be like all the nations, that our king may judge us and go out before us and fight our battles.'"

II. THE REIGN OF SAUL (1 SAMUEL 9–15)

A. Saul was Israel's <u>FIRST</u> king.

B. Saul was anointed by Samuel but chosen by <u>MEN</u>. (1 Samuel 12:12–13)

FIRST SAMUEL
Theme: The Monarchy Established

Samuel 9–12

- Saul started well as a king, from appearance to actions.
    - ~ His physique was impressive for he was taller and more handsome than others.
    - ~ He was able to unite the twelve tribes to fight and win a battle against the Ammonites.
    - ~ This was what the people had wanted—a king to fight their battles.

- All was NOT well for the people; they knew in their hearts that God was to be their king.

<table>
<tr><td>

✝ **1 Samuel 12:19** "Then all the people said to Samuel, 'Pray for your servants to the Lord your God, so that we may not die, for we have added to all our sins this evil by asking for ourselves a king.'"

</td><td>

★ TEACHING TIP:

*It is important to remember the "sin cycle." Any **rebellion** (rejection) against God was followed by God's **rejection**.*

</td></tr>
</table>

⇨ **Be careful what you pray for—you might get it. The Israelites now had a human king.**

1 Samuel 13

- The Philistines were still active enemies with iron weapons and 30,000 chariots.
- When the Israelites saw the Philistines approaching them, they ran and hid in caves.
- Samuel told Saul to go to Gilgal and stay there for seven days while he sought God to learn what God wanted Saul to do.
- Saul waited seven days, but Samuel had not returned, so with the Israelites scattering and the Philistines coming, Saul decided to act on his **own** (without direction from God).
    - ~ Even though Saul was <u>not</u> a priest, he took an animal and sacrificed it.

⇨ **"On his own," Saul acted in total disobedience.**

C. Saul was disqualified by God for his <u>UNFAITHFULNESS</u>.

- Saul, in reality, disqualified himself to remain the king of Israel.

✝ **1 Samuel 13:13–14** "Samuel said to Saul, 'You have acted foolishly; you have not kept the commandment of the Lord your God, which He commanded you, for now the Lord would have established your kingdom over Israel forever. But now your kingdom shall not endure. The Lord has sought out for Himself a man after His own heart, and the Lord has appointed him as ruler over His people, because you have not kept what the Lord commanded you.'"

- His first act of disobedience was presumptuously acting as a priest, but this would not be his last.

✞ **1 Samuel 15:2–3** "Thus says the Lord of hosts, 'I will punish Amalek for what he did to Israel, how he set himself against him on the way while he was coming up from Egypt. Now go and strike Amalek and utterly destroy all that he has, and do not spare him; but put to death both man and woman, child and infant, ox and sheep, camel and donkey.'"

> ★ **TEACHING TIP:**
>
> *We must study Scripture in light of Scripture. God states in 2 Peter 3:9 that He is not willing that any should perish. Knowing this about God we can trust that He had given the Amalekites every opportunity to get right with Him.*

> **NOTE:** This command from God could be disconcerting. Why would God instruct that children and animals be killed? It is important to understand who the Amalekites were:
> * They were descendants of Esau, Jacob's brother. (Genesis 36:16)
> * They tried to destroy Israel when they came out of Egypt. (Exodus 17:8-16)
> * The Israelites had been told before going into the Promised Land to blot out Amalek (this was something they were not to forget), because the Amalekites did not fear God and attacked His people when they were exhausted. (Deuteronomy 25:17–19)
> ⇨ **The Amalekites had a long history of being God's enemies, and they were bent on destroying Israel.**

> ❖ **APPLICATION:** We have some enemies in our personal lives that we should not live with, such as anger, bitterness, an unforgiving heart, or coveting. Such enemies must be utterly destroyed.

✞ **1 Samuel 15:9** "But Saul and the people spared Agag and the best of the sheep, the oxen, the fatlings, the lambs, and all that was good, and were not willing to destroy them utterly; but everything despised and worthless, that they utterly destroyed."

- What had God commanded? Destroy ALL. When God said this He meant "all!"
- Saul decided (along with the people) to destroy only what they despised and deemed worthless.
- They kept the best of the livestock and also SPARED the Amalekite king's life!

FIRST SAMUEL
Theme: The Monarchy Established

⇨ **This principle has been stated before: partial obedience IS disobedience!**

1 Samuel 15:20–21

- Saul claimed that he had obeyed God; but the Amalekite king was alive.
- He blamed the people for sparing the best animals and stated these animals were to be used "as a sacrifice to God."

> **NOTE:** Consider for a moment Saul's response.
> - First, he lied about destroying all the people knowing full well that he had not— the king was still alive.
> - Then he blamed the people for taking the best animals. Didn't we see a similar "blame-game" with Adam? Essentially Saul was stating that this situation was not his fault! But he was the king, their leader!
> - Finally, he tried to justify their disobedience by bringing God into his rationale— they were going to use the animals that they kept for a sacrifice to God.

- God's response was direct. Paraphrased: "I did not ask for a sacrifice; I asked for obedience."

✟ **1 Samuel 15:22–23** "Samuel said, 'Has the Lord as much delight in burnt offerings and sacrifices As in obeying the voice of the Lord? Behold, to obey is better than sacrifice, And to heed than the fat of rams. 'For rebellion is as the sin of divination, And insubordination is as iniquity and idolatry. Because you have rejected the word of the Lord, He has also rejected you from being king.'"

- God defined their rebellion as the same as worshipping an idol!

> ❖ **APPLICATION:** We do not think of ourselves as idol worshipers: but in God's economy we are when we rebel against Him for we are putting something <u>before</u> Him. Disobedience reveals this.

- God explained the choice and stated the consequences of Saul's disobedience:
    - ~ **The Choice:** In his disobedience, Saul had rejected the word of the Lord.
    - ~ God had clearly told Saul what to do with the Amalekites.
    - ~ **The Consequence:** God would reject him from being king.

- In 1 Samuel 28 we see God's rejection of Saul come to fruition:

✟ **1 Samuel 28:17** "The Lord has done accordingly as He spoke through me; for the Lord has torn the kingdom out of your hand and given it to your neighbor, to David."

D. He sought guidance from a <u>MEDIUM</u> and not from God.

<u>1 Samuel 28</u>

> ❖ **APPLICATION:** Saul had God Almighty as his resource for direction, yet he sought a medium!
>   - ~ With the popularity of zodiac signs, horoscopes, crystals, and such, this can also be a pitfall for us, as believers.
>   - ~ Do not seek counterfeit direction when you have the Holy Spirit as your God-given, authentic teacher and guide!

E. Saul <u>DIED</u> after forty years as king of Israel.

<u>Samuel 29–31</u>

> ★ **TEACHING TIP:**
> *Israel had demanded a king because they had unfaithful hearts. Saul was rejected as king because he had an unfaithful heart.*

- The Philistines ultimately overtook Saul. His sons were killed, and he was wounded.
- Saul asked his armor bearer to kill him, but his servant refused.
- King Saul fell on his own sword and died.

⇨ **God has a faithful heart, and He is looking for people with a heart like His.**

III. THE FAITHFULNESS OF DAVID, GOD'S CHOSEN KING (1 SAMUEL 16–31)

- "Now the Lord said to Samuel, 'How long will you grieve over Saul, since I have rejected him from being king over Israel? Fill your horn with oil and go; I will send you to Jesse the Bethlehemite, for I have selected a king for Myself among His sons.'" (1 Samuel 16:1–2)
- Because of his faithfulness to God, Samuel went to Bethlehem.
- He first met Jesse's oldest son and assumed that he would be the next king chosen by God.

<u>REVIEW</u>:

- ⌖ **The Memory Verse:** "But the Lord said to Samuel, 'Do not look at his appearance or at the height of his stature, because I have rejected him; for God sees not as man sees, for man looks at the outward appearance, but the Lord looks at the heart.'" (1 Samuel 16:7)

FIRST SAMUEL
Theme: The Monarchy Established

A. David was anointed as Israel's king <u>ELECT</u>.

B. He was anointed by Samuel but chosen by <u>GOD</u>.

- Man looks at the outward appearance of a man—his natural abilities, physique, clothing, etc.
  - ~ So Samuel thought the eldest son of Jesse was the logical choice.
- God, however, looks at the heart of a man and his character.
  - ~ God chose Jesse's youngest son, David.
    - ~ The great-grandson of Ruth and Boaz, the kinsman-redeemer.

✟ **1 Samuel 16:13** "Then Samuel took the horn of oil and anointed him in the midst of his brothers; and the Spirit of the Lord came mightily upon David from that day forward."

- David was anointed as "king elect." He was not ruling yet; Saul was still the king.

C. He was qualified to be king by his <u>FAITHFULNESS</u>.

- David's faithfulness was demonstrated by how he served King Saul.

✟ **1 Samuel 16:14** "Now the Spirit of the Lord departed from Saul, and an evil spirit from the Lord terrorized him."

> **NOTE:** This can be a troublesome verse if we do not understand a few things:
> - ◆ The word "terrorized" used here means "made miserable, distressed or unhappy."
> - ◆ Before Jesus came to die, the Holy Spirit would come upon people to use them for God's purposes. When their job for the Lord was completed, the Spirit might leave them.
>   - ~ With the coming of Christ and His sacrifice for us, the Holy Spirit comes into us, seals us, and promises never to leave us.
> - ◆ If God's Spirit left Saul, the only thing left would have been Saul's own spirit or evil spirits causing him misery, distress, and unhappiness.

⇨ **Without God in him, Saul was troubled by evil but David faithfully played music to soothe him.**

D. David sought <u>GOD</u> and lived.

E. David trusted God and killed the Philistine <u>GIANT</u>, Goliath.

1 Samuel 17

- One of the best known stories about David is in this chapter.
- Israel now had Saul, a king who rebelled against God.
- Their enemy, the Philistines, remained in active opposition to the Israelites; they now had a giant warrior named Goliath.
- Goliath was over nine feet tall and had 200 pounds of armor plus a javelin with a twenty pound point.
- He was ready for a fight and dared the Israelites:"Choose a man for yourselves and let him come down to me. If he is able to fight with me and kill me, then we will become your servants; but if I prevail against him and kill him, then you shall become our servants and serve us." (1 Samuel 17:8b–9)
- The Israelites were afraid of Goliath. No one volunteered to fight him.
- During this time, David's brothers were fighting in the war and his father sent him with provisions for his brothers.
- David, a young man, asked a question, "For who is this uncircumcised Philistine, that he should taunt the armies of the living God?" (1 Samuel 17:26b)
- He then volunteered to fight Goliath, but Saul said he was too young to engage in such a fight.
- David responded to Saul's suggestion that his age disqualified him from fighting Goliath:

✝ **1 Samuel 17:37** "And David said, 'The Lord who delivered me from the paw of the lion and from the paw of the bear, He will deliver me from the hand of this Philistine.'"

- Then David spoke directly to Goliath:

✝ **1 Samuel 17:45** "You come to me with a sword, a spear, and a javelin, but I come to you in the name of the Lord of hosts, the God of the armies of Israel, whom you have taunted."

❖ **APPLICATION:** What giant are you facing today?
   ~ When faced with giant problems, we need to remember the times God protected us from smaller enemies and praise Him.
   ~ Then we need to trust that if God could take care of our small problems, He can take care of the giants in our life, as well.

F. There was an ongoing conflict between <u>MAN'S</u> king, Saul, and <u>GOD'S</u> king, David.

- The remainder of 1 Samuel is about the conflict between Saul and David.

- It also speaks to the extremely close relationship between Saul's son, Jonathan, and David.

G. David had a covenant relationship with Saul's son, Jonathan.

1 Samuel 18–19

- Because Jonathan was the rightful heir to the throne, he could have easily been jealous that David was the anointed king, yet he loved David as he loved himself.
- They made a covenant with one another. Jonathan promised that he would warn David if his father made plans to kill him.

1 Samuel 22

- David ran for his life and hid in caves with an army of approximately 400 men. His army was not what one would expect: "Everyone who was in distress ... in debt ... and ... discontented gathered to him." (1 Samuel 22:2)
  - ~ Obviously this was not a strong, well-trained army!!

✟ **1 Samuel 23:15–16** "Now David became aware that Saul had come out to seek his life while David was in the wilderness ... And Jonathan, Saul's son, arose and went to David and encouraged him in God."

- David needed a friend who could get his focus off the problem and back on God.
- What a faithful friend Jonathan was!

1 Samuel 30:3–6

- David returned with his men to Ziklag (the city in which he lived) and found that it had been invaded and burned by the Amalekites.
- They also found that the Amalekites had taken captive their wives, sons, and daughters.
- The response of those returning was overwhelming grief. Scripture states that they wept until they had no more strength to weep.

> **NOTE:** Could this devastation, captivity, and heart-wrenching grief have been avoided?
> - What had God instructed Saul in regards to the Amalekites?
> - He had said that they were to be completely destroyed.
> - But Saul had only "partially" destroyed this enemy.
> - Because this enemy was not dealt with as God had commanded, the Amalekites were able to "regroup," attack, and take captive Israelite victims.
>
> ⇨ **What a tragic consequence of not fully obeying God!**

- The people's grief turned into an angry bitterness that produced discussions of stoning David for what had happened to their sons and daughters!
- This antagonistic attitude of the people distressed David, yet he kept his focus where it needed to be: "...But David strengthened himself in the Lord his God." (1 Samuel 30:6b)
  ~ David had a faithful friend who had encouraged him in God so that later he was able to encourage himself.

⇨ ## PICTURES OF JESUS IN 1 SAMUEL

1. Jesus is the true prophet, high priest and judge.

- Samuel is a type or picture of Jesus in his role as a prophet, priest, and judge.
- ✝ **Mark 6:4** "Jesus said to them, 'A prophet is not without honor except in his hometown and among his own relatives and in his own household.'"
- ✝ **Luke 24:19** "And they said to Him, 'The things about Jesus the Nazarene, who was a prophet mighty in deed and word in the sight of God and all the people ...'"
- ✝ **Hebrews 4:14** "Therefore, since we have a great high priest who has passed through the heavens, Jesus the Son of God, let us hold fast our confession."
- ✝ **John 5:22–23** "For not even the Father judges anyone, but He has given all judgment to the Son, so that all will honor the Son even as they honor the Father. He who does not honor the Son does not honor the Father who sent Him." *(Familiarize yourself with entire passage of vv22–30)*

2. Jesus is the King of kings.

- David is a clear picture of Jesus: great-grandson of Boaz (the kinsman-redeemer), born in Bethlehem, a shepherd, Israel's greatest king, rejected, and in danger as his enemies threatened his life.
- In 1 Samuel, David was anointed king but was not yet reigning. Jesus has been anointed and is coming to reign as King of kings.

FINAL THOUGHTS AND APPLICATION

- ¤ The people demanded that they have a king like the other nations, yet they were never meant to be like other nations. They were God's chosen people to be different and set apart to Him.
- ¤ The New Testament tells us, as believers, that Jesus is the only King of kings and Lord of lords. (1 Timothy 6:14–15)

> ❖ **APPLICATION:** Is Jesus your King? Are you being faithful to your King?
>
> ⇨ Remember—*partial obedience **is** disobedience.*

⌻ Jonathan is an example of a true, godly friend. He encouraged David to look up to God Who was greater than any circumstance he may face.

> ❖ **APPLICATION:** What kind of friend are you? Do you encourage others in the Lord, so that they can one day encourage themselves?

❖ **FINAL APPLICATION:** Jesus is the King of kings. Is He reigning as King over your life, or are you demanding another king?

FIRST SAMUEL
Theme: The Monarchy Established

FIRST SAMUEL REVIEW HELPS

1. What was the main historical event in the book of Joshua?

2. Who became the leader of Israel after Moses death?

3. In the book of Joshua, what promise to Abraham by God was fulfilled?

4. Where does the book of Joshua take place?

5. The book of Judges records seven _____.

6. Who were three famous judges?

7. What did a judge do in the book of Judges?

8. What judge had extraordinary strength?

9. What judge was a woman?

10. What judge was afraid and hid in the winepress?

11. In what country did the book of Ruth begin?

12. What two words describe the role Boaz played in Ruth's life that is the theme of the book?

13. What famous king was Ruth's great-grandson?

14. The book of Ruth takes place during what historical book?

FIRST SAMUEL REVIEW HELPS
(Answers for Facilitators)

1. What was the main historical event in the book of Joshua? **Conquering the land**

2. Who became the leader of Israel after Moses death? **Joshua**

3. In the book of Joshua, what promise to Abraham by God was fulfilled? **Land**

4. Where does the book of Joshua take place? **Canaan**

5. The book of Judges records seven **Sin Cycles**.

6. Who were three famous judges? **Deborah, Gideon, Samson**

7. What did a judge do in the book of Judges? **He led the people into battle**

8. What judge had extraordinary strength? **Samson**

9. What judge was a woman? **Deborah**

10. What judge was afraid and hid in the winepress? **Gideon**

11. In what country did the book of Ruth begin? **Moab**

12. What two words describe the role Boaz played in Ruth's life that are the theme of the book? **Kinsman-Redeemer**

13. What famous king was Ruth's great-grandson? **David**

14. The book of Ruth takes place during what historical book? **Judges**

SECOND SAMUEL

David's Throne Established

*May the house of Your servant David
be established before You.*

2 Samuel 7:26

SESSION TEN: SECOND SAMUEL
David's Throne Established

✝ **Memory Verse:** "*... may the house of Your servant David be established before You.*" (*2 Samuel 7:26*)

- **Introduction:** In 1 Samuel, Saul had been crowned king and reigned for forty years, failing miserably to establish Israel as a secure and united nation. In 2 Samuel, David became king and united the kingdom, conquered their enemies, and brought the people back to their God. God promised him He would establish his throne forever.

- **Oral Review:** Please refer to the **REVIEW Section** in the following Teaching Guide Outline.

- **Homework:** Review the homework for 1 Samuel. The following are key questions to be discussed.

    The question on the bottom of page 105
    The questions on page 108–109
    The question on the 110–111
    All questions on page 114

- **Review Helps:** Written review is provided at the end of the teachers' presentation. (Optional and time permitting.)

- **Teacher Presentation on the Book of 2 Samuel**

- **Learning for Life Discussion questions:** You may choose to discuss all or just one or two of the questions on page 127.

- **Closing prayer:** Pray that the participant would have a heart after God and that unity would reign in their families.

TEACHER NOTE: Now would be a good time to order workbooks for Set Three.

SECOND SAMUEL
Theme: David's Throne Established

TIMELINE AID FOR TEACHERS:

- **2 Samuel 1–10   The Triumphs of David**
  - ~ David lamented the death of Saul and Jonathan
  - ~ David reigned over Judah at Hebron
  - ~ David reigned over Israel (twelve tribes)
  - ~ David's throne was established in Jerusalem
  - ~ The ark was brought to Jerusalem
  - ~ God made a covenant with David (Davidic covenant)
  - ~ David was victorious in battles
  - ~ David showed kindness to Mephibosheth
  - ~ There was conflict with the Ammonites and Arameans

- **2 Samuel 11–24 The Troubles of David**
  - ~ David sinned against Bathsheba, Uriah, and the Lord
  - ~ Amnon raped Tamar
  - ~ Absalom murdered Amnon
  - ~ Absalom fled Jerusalem
  - ~ Absalom returned to Jerusalem
  - ~ Absalom conspired against David
  - ~ David fled Jerusalem
  - ~ Absalom was defeated
  - ~ David was reinstated as king
  - ~ David avenged the Gibeonites
  - ~ David took a census
  - ~ David stopped the plague and offered a sacrifice at Araunah's threshing floor

2 SAMUEL
[David's Throne Established]

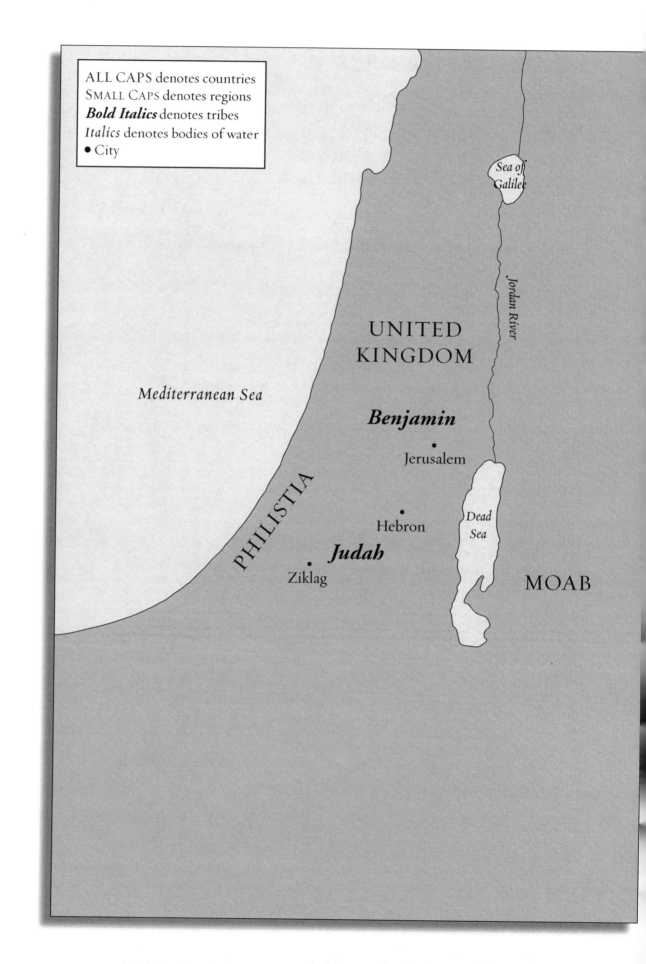

ALL CAPS denotes countries
SMALL CAPS denotes regions
Bold Italics denotes tribes
Italics denotes bodies of water
● City

Sea of Galilee

Jordan River

UNITED KINGDOM

Mediterranean Sea

Benjamin

● Jerusalem

PHILISTIA

Dead Sea

● Hebron

Judah

● Ziklag

MOAB

SECOND SAMUEL
Theme: David's Throne Established

THE BASICS:
⇨ **Who: The Author:** Believed to have been written by Samuel with additions written by the prophets, Gad and Nathan

      Main Character: David

⇨ **What:** David establishes the monarchy

⇨ **When:** The book covers forty-four years (1011-971 B.C.)

⇨ **Where:** In Chapters 1–4, David is king over Judah. In Chapters 5–24, David is king over all the tribes in one nation (Israel).

⇨ **Why:** Through David's leadership all the tribes of Israel were united into one great nation.

MEMORY VERSE: *"... may the house of Your servant David be established before You."*
2 Samuel 7:26

****

REVIEW:
THE PENTATEUCH
⌑ Began with the creation of the world, the fall of man, God's judgment of the world through a flood, and the beginning of languages and nations.

⌑ God gave Abraham three promises:
1. His descendants would become a great nation.
2. They would be given a special land.
3. One descendant would be a blessing to the whole world.

⌑ The people grew in number while slaves in Egypt.

⌑ God chose Moses to deliver His people from Egypt, and Moses led them to the edge of the Promised Land.

THE KINGDOM BOOKS
JOSHUA
⌑ Joshua took the Israelites into the land.

⌑ They conquered and divided it among the twelve tribes.

JUDGES
⌑ Covered the 340 years that the people were a theocracy led by judges.

⌑ The judges were sent by God to rescue them when they did what was right in their own eyes.

⌑ This "satisfying self" mindset of the people led them into a sin cycle: Israel rebelled > God rejected > Israel repented > God rescued > Israel rested—until they rebelled yet again.

SECOND SAMUEL
Theme: David's Throne Established

RUTH
- ⌑ Took place during the dark time of the judges.
- ⌑ Gave hope for a coming kinsman-redeemer.

1 SAMUEL
- ⌑ The kingdom was established when the people demanded a king.
- ⌑ Saul became the first king.
    - ~ Under his leadership, the nation suffered greatly and was worse off upon his death than when he began his reign.
    - ~ The religious system was weakened.
    - ~ He never established a strong government, so the nation of twelve tribes was never truly united.
- ⌑ David was anointed by God to be the next king even as Saul reigned.
- ⌑ Because of Saul's jealousy, David had to run for his life and live as a refugee.
- ⌑ At the end of 1 Samuel, Saul fell on his own sword and died in battle. The nation was in great turmoil as the armies of Israel had been devastated by the Philistines.

OVERVIEW:

- In 2 Samuel, Israel at last received a "leader." One who would unite the kingdom, lead the people spiritually, have courage and faith to trust God in battles, and secure peace and prosperity for the nation.
- The entire book is devoted to the reign of King David, Israel's greatest king and an ancestor of Jesus Christ.
- David loved God passionately, humbled himself under God's authority, and was a man after God's own heart—and yet, he sinned.
- The success of David's life was tarnished but not erased by the consequences of his sin.
- When David united the tribes, three things took place that set this nation apart:
    1. They began to work as one nation, helping each other for the benefit of all.
    2. They established a central place of worship that was for all the tribes.
    3. They brought glory to God because they were "different" from the surrounding nations as they lived in obedience and together worshiped one God.

- Second Samuel is believed to have been written by Samuel with additions written by the prophets, Gad and Nathan.
- The main character is David as king. It covers forty years of his reign, seven as he reigned over Judah alone and thirty-three years as king of all of Israel's twelve tribes.
- Saul was king for forty years, David was king for forty years, and Solomon, David's son, reigned for forty years as well.

SECOND SAMUEL
Theme: David's Throne Established

⇨ **The purpose of 2 Samuel is to continue the history of Israel during the reign of King David.**

I. DAVID <u>TRIUMPHED</u> IN UNITING THE TWELVE TRIBES OF ISRAEL (2 SAMUEL 1–10)

- The first ten chapters deal with the very best years of David's life because he was blessed greatly by God, Who was with him wherever he went.

2 Samuel 1
- David received word that Saul had been killed.
- Even though Saul had been trying to kill him for many years, David grieved over Saul's death.

2 Samuel 2:1–7
- David was living in Ziklag in Philistine territory when he sought God's guidance as to what he should do next.
- He knew he had been anointed king, but he waited on God's perfect timing.
- The Lord told David to go to Hebron in Judah, and David obeyed. He took all of his men with him.
- Upon his arrival in Hebron, the people of Judah asked him to be their king.

A. David ruled only one tribe, <u>JUDAH</u>, for seven years.
2 Samuel 2:5-11
- Even though God had promised that he would be king over all of Israel, God did not give David all twelve tribes immediately after Saul's death.

B. David <u>UNITED</u> the twelve tribes after the death of Saul's son.
- The northern tribes had a different king. His name was Ish-Bosheth, and he was Saul's son.
- For seven years, Judah was under the leadership of King David while the northern tribes were led by Saul's son.
- Ish-Bosheth was a weak leader who did not have the strength to unite the kingdom. These northern tribes became weaker and weaker.
- After seven years Ish-Bosheth was murdered and all of the northern tribes asked David to be their king, thus fulfilling the words God had given to Samuel in 1 Samuel 16:1–13.

SECOND SAMUEL
Theme: David's Throne Established

1. He established <u>JERUSALEM</u> as the capital of Israel. (2 Samuel 5)

- The first act David did, after being crowned king, was to conquer Jerusalem.
- Jerusalem should have been taken by Joshua 400 years before, but it had stayed under the control of the Jebusites.
- There were a couple of problems with conquering Jerusalem:
  - **Its location**: Even though the Israelites were living all around Jerusalem, they were never able to conquer it because it was situated on a hill which made it easy for the Jebusites to see the enemy coming.
  - **Its wall**: It was surrounded by a great wall—a fortress that the people felt they could not take.
- The Jebusites in Jerusalem felt quite safe and secure. When they saw David with his men approaching the city, they hung over the wall and taunted them.

✞ **2 Samuel 5:6** "... You shall not come in here, but the blind and lame will turn you away ..."

> ★ **TEACHING TIP:**
> *It is an interesting choice of words in suggesting that the "blind" would turn David away! It appears that the Jebusites had a "blind spot" when they forgot Who was behind David! Because David was a great man with an awesome God!*

- Undaunted by the Jebusites' taunting, David and his men came into Jerusalem through the water system and quickly conquered it.
- He established Jerusalem as the capital over the twelve tribes because it was more centrally located than Hebron in the south, allowing him to more easily care for and control all of the tribes.

⇨ **It is interesting to note that, even today, Jerusalem still plays a central and important role in world events.**

2. He established a strong <u>RELIGIOUS</u> order. (2 Samuel 6)

- After David established a central place for government rule, he brought the ark to Jerusalem.
- Saul had so weakened the religious system that it was almost totally decimated.
- David, a man after God's own heart, knew it was critical to hold the tribes together through their love and faith in God.
- When he brought the ark into Jerusalem, there was a glorious celebration.
- David, the king and mighty warrior, danced joyfully before the Lord and the people because he was grateful to a mighty God Who had not forgotten His promises.

3. He expanded the <u>BORDERS</u> of Israel. (2 Samuel 8-10)

- As king, David began to establish military strength by building up his army.
- Other great nations (the Philistines, Moabites, and Edomites) attacked Israel, but David led his people to victory.
- With these victories, Israel gained more land and control.
- David never lost a battle because his God was with him wherever he went.

⇨ **David established the religious order, a capital city, and a solid government. He united all the tribes.**

4. God made a <u>COVENANT</u> with King David. (2 Samuel 7)

- God spoke to David and gave him some incredible promises.

✞ **2 Samuel 7:9** "I have been with you wherever you have gone and have cut off all your enemies from before you; and I will make you a great name, like the names of the great men who are on the earth."

- The first thing God gave him was victory over his enemies.
- The second promise was a great name among the names of other great men.

> ★ **TEACHING TIP:**
> *About 3,000 years have passed since King David walked on this earth, yet, he is known throughout the world to this day! God said it, and He brought it about.*

- David had unbelievable successes wherever he went. He gave honor and glory to God alone for he knew it was God Who made him successful.
- His response to God's promises showed his great humility:

✞ **2 Samuel 7:18b, 22** "Who am I, O Lord God, and what is my house, that You have brought me this far? ... there is none like You, and there is no God besides You, according to all that we have heard with our ears."

⇨ **Though David was the king of Israel, he realized that there was a King far greater Who had all power and wisdom.**

- David's life took a sudden and unfortunate turn. His success was interrupted as he made a decision that would change the rest of his life and the rest of history.

> ★ **TEACHING TIP:**
> *The consequences of sin are easily seen, yet sometimes we simply refuse to believe they can be so horrific. But God is adamant that sin can ruin and even destroy us. His love for His people is so great that He commands us to live in holiness instead of sin.*

> ❖ **APPLICATION:** It is interesting how one sinful choice can do that.
>   ~ A beautiful young girl, full of life and energy with a promising future, climbs into the back seat of a car and in that one night becomes pregnant, and her life changes forever.
>   ~ Or the man who works in an office with an attractive woman, engages in an affair with her, and loses his family and job.
>   ~ Sin can do this. One bad choice can devastate many lives, often those they love the most.

II. DAVID <u>TRANSGRESSED</u> AGAINST GOD. (2 SAMUEL 11-12)

A. David committed <u>ADULTERY</u> with Bathsheba.

- All of the warriors had gone off to war in the spring, and he should have been with them, but he stayed home in the king's house.
- This great man, at the age of forty, looked over the wall and saw a beautiful woman— and he wanted her. Her name was Bathsheba.
  ~ He took her into his house, and he took her sexually.
- Tragically this marked the beginning of David's moral, downward spiral into deep sin.

- Bathsheba became pregnant. When she told David, he saw only one way out of this "situation," which involved deceit.
  ~ Bathsheba was married to Uriah, one of David's mighty warriors. Uriah was loyal to David and ready to die for him.
  ~ David brought Uriah back from the battlefield with a plan for Uriah to go home to Bathsheba to have relations with her.
  ~ David wined and dined Uriah, then commanded him to go home and have time with his wife.
- David had one goal: a cover-up! He wanted the people to think the baby that Bathsheba carried was Uriah's, not his.
- However, Uriah, a good man, refused to go home to have time with his wife and enjoy her company. In his mind, how could he spend time with his wife when the ark and his mighty men were on the front lines of battle, living and sleeping in the open field?

✝ **2 Samuel 11:11b** "Shall I then go to my house to eat and to drink and to lie with my wife? By your life and the life of your soul, I will not do this thing."

- David tried yet again to get Uriah drunk and send him home to lie with Bathsheba, but Uriah continued to refuse to go home.

SECOND SAMUEL
Theme: David's Throne Established

B. David **MURDERED** Uriah.

- Surmising that he only had one option, David did the unthinkable—he had Uriah killed on the front lines.

⇨ **David's sin had spiraled out of control. He went from being a great man of God to being an adulterer and a murderer.**

- He brought Bathsheba into his house, and she became his wife.
- And a baby, a son, was born.

C. The prophet **NATHAN** confronted David with his sin.

2 Samuel 12:1-15

- After the baby was born, God sent the prophet Nathan to David.
- Nathan told David a story that illustrated to David the depths of his own sin.
    - ~ The story involved a poor man wronged by a rich man.
        - ⋆ The poor man had one lamb. It had grown up with his children, thus was loved.
        - ⋆ Even though the rich man had many flocks and herds, he took the poor man's lamb, killed it, and served it while entertaining a friend.
    - ~ Thinking that Nathan's story was true, David responded with anger toward the rich man's actions and stated that the man deserved to die for what he had done.
    - ~ Nathan informed him that he (David) was the rich man, and Uriah was the poor man. David had many wives, yet he took Uriah's one wife and then had him killed on the battlefield while serving King David.
- Through the application of Nathan's story, David came face-to-face with the ugliness and brutality of his own sin.

D. David **CONFESSED** and repented of his sin before God.

- David, as the king, could have killed Nathan. Instead his response was: "… I have sinned against the Lord." (2 Samuel 12:13)
- It is important to see that David did not say that he had sinned against Bathsheba or even Uriah. He acknowledged that God was the supreme judge and ruler, thus his sin was first and foremost against Him.

2 Samuel 12:10-12, 14

- God said that he would forgive David's sin, BUT the consequences of that sin would stand.
    - ~ The sword would never leave his house.
    - ~ Evil would rise up against his household.

~ Another man would have David's wives before his eyes in broad daylight.

~ His child with Bathsheba would die.

⇨ **From this point on, David lived a life of great sorrow.**

- The first part of David's life was a life of great success. In the middle of his life, he sinned. He lived in sorrow during the last part of his life. It is a sad story of a great man.

III. DAVID SUFFERED <u>TROUBLES</u> FROM THE CONSEQUENCES OF HIS SIN. (2 SAMUEL 13-21)

A. David's infant <u>SON</u> died. (2 Samuel 12)

- David begged God for his son's life, but the child died because of David's sin.
- The tragedy in David's family continued bringing even more sorrow.

B. David's son Amnon <u>SEDUCED</u> his half-sister Tamar and then raped her. (2 Samuel 13)

<u>2 Samuel 13:1-19</u>

- His grown son, Amnon, fell in love with David's grown daughter, Tamar.
- Even though Tamar begged him not to, Amnon brutally raped her.
- Before he raped her, he loved her, but afterward he was disgusted with her and threw her out of the room.
- Tamar lived in seclusion the remainder of her life.

⇨ **This would be a tragedy for any family, yet these were the consequences of David's sin. David had committed adultery, and his son took it further by committing rape and incest.**

C. Tamar's brother, Absalom, <u>MURDERED</u> Amnon.

<u>2 Samuel 13:20-33</u>

- Two years after the rape of his sister, Absalom took his revenge for her.
- In great anger for what Amnon had done, Absalom murdered him in cold blood.

⇨ **David murdered Uriah, his loyal and faithful subject. Absalom murdered his own brother. Again, there were tragic consequences for David's sin.**

<u>2 Samuel 13:34–38</u>

- Absalom ran for his life and lived in Geshur for three years.

D. Absalom led a <u>REVOLT</u> against his father, David. (2 Samuel 15–18)

<u>2 Samuel 15:1–12</u>

- He came back to Jerusalem and began to woo the people with his charm.
- He manipulated them to agree that he would be a better leader than David and convinced them to crown him as their king.
- From there, he led a revolt against his father, King David.

<u>2 Samuel 15:13–17:29</u>

- David and all the people who were still loyal to him fled for their lives, leaving the city of Jerusalem.
- David had been king for forty years, but became a fugitive running from his own son who sought to kill him.
- The loyal priests brought the ark out to David, but he told them to take it back.

✝ **2 Samuel 15:25-26** "… Return the ark of God to the city. If I find favor in the sight of the Lord, then He will bring me back again and show me both it and His habitation. But if He should say thus, 'I have no delight in you,' behold, here I am, let Him do to me as seems good to Him."

⇨ **David was a man totally surrendered to the will of God. No matter how painful it would be, he was willing to do God's will even at the cost of losing the kingdom.**

E. Absalom was <u>MURDERED</u> by David's army commander.

<u>2 Samuel 18</u>

- God brought David back to Jerusalem after the death of Absalom, who was murdered by Joab.

REVIEW:

- ¤ David lost two of his sons to murder, his daughter was raped, and his infant son had died.
- ¤ There had been a sword in his household all these days.
- ¤ God had said this would happen and it did.

IV. DAVID TESTIFIED TO THE FAITHFULNESS OF GOD. (2 SAMUEL 22-24)

A. In success, he praised God.

B. In sin, he repented before God.

C. In sorrow, he clung to God.

D. He was a man after God's own heart.

- At the end of 2 Samuel, David still testified to the faithfulness of his God.

✞ **2 Samuel 22:2–3** "The Lord is my rock and my fortress and my deliverer; My God, my rock, in whom I take refuge, My shield and the horn of my salvation, my stronghold and my refuge; My savior …"

- David was a man who praised God in his great success. In his sin, he repented before God. And in his sorrow, he clung to God.

⇨ **In success, sin, and sorrow, David sought God.**

2 Samuel 24:1-14

- The book of 2 Samuel ends on a sad note with a short story relating how once again David sinned.
- David took a census and in doing so, he put his faith in the number of his warriors rather than in his God.

2 Samuel 24:15-25

- Consequences followed this sin: God brought a great plague on the land.
  - ~ 70,000 men of the people from Dan to Beersheba died.
- Jerusalem was the next city to be impacted by this plague.
- David once again recognized his sin.

✞ **2 Samuel 24:17** "Then David spoke to the Lord … 'Behold, it is I who have sinned, and it is I who have done wrong … Please let Your hand be against me and against my father's house.'"

- David was instructed to buy a threshing floor and build an altar upon it. If he did as told, God would stop the plague. David obeyed.

> **NOTE:** The threshing floor that David bought was the same site upon which Abraham offered Isaac to God. It was also the very site upon which Solomon built his temple. And it is the same site that receives much attention and conflict today.

⇨ **David was a king, a musician, and a poet; but more than anything else, he was a man with a heart for God.**

⇨ ## PICTURES OF JESUS IN 2 SAMUEL

1. Jesus is the King of kings with an eternal kingdom.

SECOND SAMUEL
Theme: David's Throne Established

- In 2 Samuel 7:16 God told David, "Your house and your kingdom shall endure before Me forever; your throne shall be established forever."
  - ~ Forever includes eternity so, through David, we have Jesus Christ beautifully pictured.
- ✝ **Luke 1:31–33** "And behold, you will conceive in your womb and bear a son, and you shall name Him Jesus. He will be great and will be called the Son of the Most High; and the Lord God will give Him the throne of His father David; and He will reign over the house of Jacob forever, and His kingdom will have no end."
  - ~ These are the words of the angel to the virgin Mary, informing her she would have a son.
- ✝ **Matthew 1:1** "The record of the genealogy of Jesus the Messiah, the son of David, the son of Abraham ..."

⇨ **Jesus was a descendant of David whose throne God established and gave to Jesus Christ for all eternity. Again, God said it, therefore He will bring it about.**

FINAL THOUGHTS AND APPLICATION

- ⌑ David's life is a living example to all believers regarding these two truths about sin:
  1. There are consequences for sin.
  2. Sin will impact many more lives than just the life of the sinner.
- ⌑ His life also shows us the appropriate way to respond when confronted about our sin— whether by God or others. First, he listened, but more importantly, he acknowledged the truth of what he heard.

⇨ **There is only one response that is acceptable in confronting sin: heartfelt repentance!**
  - ~ This will result in our confessing our sin, turning back to God, and walking in obedience to Him.
  - ~ This will also guide us in accepting and responding appropriately to the consequences of our sin.

> ❖ **APPLICATION:** Spend some time talking with God.
> - ~ If you are in the midst of a success, praise Him.
> - ~ If you are engaged in sin, repent before Him.
> - ~ If you are experiencing sorrow, cling to Him.

❖ **FINAL APPLICATION: God can be trusted in our triumphs, will forgive us for our transgressions, and will strengthen and encourage us in our troubles.**

SECOND SAMUEL
Theme: David's Throne Established

SECOND SAMUEL REVIEW HELPS

✧ **Purpose: To help the student match the characters with the geographical location with which they were most associated. Draw a line from the character on the left to the location on the right.**

David	Jericho
Adam	Temple
Lot	Ai
Abraham	Mt. Sinai
Achan	Sodom
Solomon	Garden of Eden
Moses	Jerusalem
Joshua	Ur
Pharaoh	Tied to pillars
Noah	Egypt
Gideon	Philistine battlefield
Saul	Ark
Samson	Winepress

SECOND SAMUEL REVIEW HELPS
(Answers for Facilitators)

✧ **Purpose: To help the student match the characters with the geographical location with which they were most associated.** *The locations are matched here with the person for the facilitator.*

David	**Jerusalem**
Adam	**Garden of Eden**
Lot	**Sodom**
Abraham	**Ur**
Achan	**Ai**
Solomon	**Temple**
Moses	**Mt. Sinai**
Joshua	**Jericho**
Pharaoh	**Egypt**
Noah	**Ark**
Gideon	**Winepress**
Saul	**Philistine battlefield**
Samson	**Tied to pillars**

FIRST KINGS

Kingdom Divided

*For when Solomon was old, his wives turned
his heart away after other gods.*

1 Kings 11:4

SESSION ELEVEN: FIRST KINGS
Kingdom Divided

✝ **Memory verse:** *"For when Solomon was old, his wives turned his heart away after other gods." (1 Kings 11:4)*

- **Introduction:** After David's death, his son Solomon became king and brought Israel into the golden years of great prosperity and peace. Yet he ended poorly as his many wives turned his heart away from God. His son Rehoboam made an unwise choice, which brought about a civil dispute that caused the ten tribes to secede from Judah. Thus Israel became the ten tribes in the north and Judah and Benjamin became Judah in the south. Elijah, God's faithful prophet, plays a key role in this book.

- **Oral Review:** Please refer to the **REVIEW Section** in the following Teaching Guide Outline.

- **Homework:** Review the homework for 2 Samuel. The following are key questions to discuss.

    Question at the top of page 133
    All questions on page 135
    Middle question on page 138
    Middle question on page 139
    Middle question on page 142

- **Review Helps:** Written review is provided at the end of the teachers' presentation. (Optional and time permitting.)

- **Teacher Presentation of the Book of 1 Kings**

- **Learning for Life Discussion questions:** You may choose to discuss all or just one or two of the questions on page 151.

- **Closing prayer:** Pray that the participants will have an undivided heart after God and that they will grow to love God and His word more deeply and profoundly as they study every book in the Bible.

First Kings
Theme: Kingdom Divided

TIMELINE AID FOR TEACHERS:

- **1 Kings 1-11   The Kingdom was UNITED**
  - ~ David died and Solomon became the king
  - ~ Solomon did an unwise thing marrying the daughter of Pharaoh
  - ~ Solomon asked God for wisdom
  - ~ God's wisdom in Solomon was demonstrated with the two women claiming one baby
  - ~ Solomon built and dedicated the temple, and God's glory filled it
  - ~ Solomon multiplied wealth, horses, and wives in disobedience to God's laws for kings
  - ~ Idol worship was the result, and God told Solomon that the kingdom would divide during his son's reign
  - ~ Solomon died

- **1 Kings 12–22   The Kingdom was DIVIDED**
  - ~ Rehoboam became the king and unwisely made life more difficult for the people
  - ~ The people revolted, and the kingdom was divided as God had predicted
  - ~ Solomon's son Rehoboam ruled the Southern Kingdom: Judah
  - ~ Jeroboam ruled the Northern Kingdom: Israel
  - ~ Jeroboam established Bethel and Dan as places of "golden calf" worship
  - ~ First Kings covers three kings in Judah: Abijam (bad), Asa (good), and Jehoshaphat (good)
  - ~ First Kings covers seven bad kings in Israel: Nadab, Baasha, Elah, Zimri, Omri, Ahab, and Ahaziah
  - ~ When Ahab became king of Israel, he and his wife, Jezebel, established Baal worship
  - ~ Elijah was a prophet in Israel during Ahab's evil reign
  - ~ Elijah prophesied a drought and famine because of the idol worship
  - ~ Elijah raised a widow's dead son to life
  - ~ Elijah challenged the 450 prophets of Baal, and God answered with fire
  - ~ Elijah ran from Jezebel and desired to die
  - ~ Jezebel murdered Naboth for his vineyard
  - ~ Ahab died

I Kings
[Kingdom Divided]

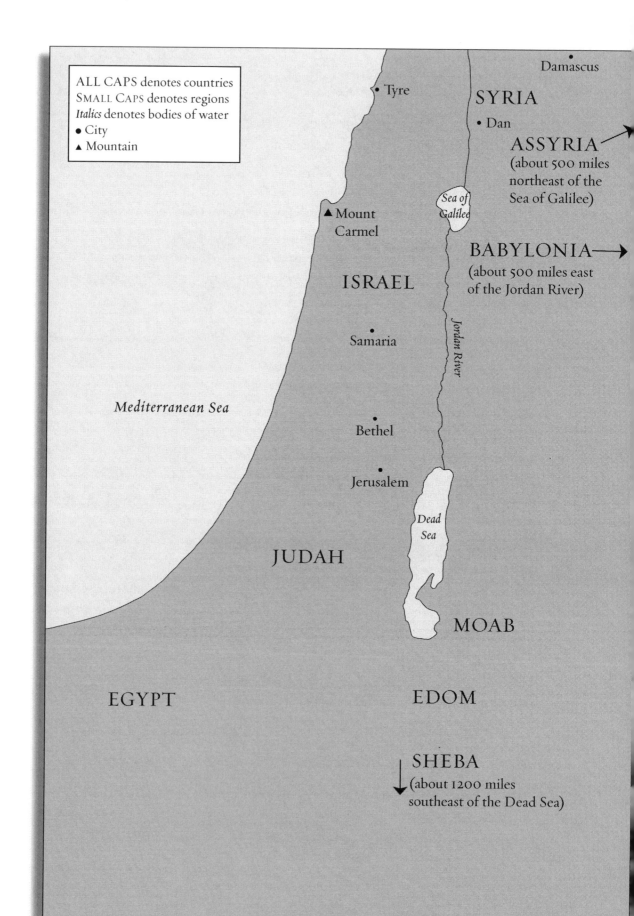

ALL CAPS denotes countries
SMALL CAPS denotes regions
Italics denotes bodies of water
● City
▲ Mountain

Damascus

• Tyre

SYRIA

• Dan

ASSYRIA
(about 500 miles
northeast of the
Sea of Galilee)

Sea of Galilee

▲ Mount
Carmel

ISRAEL

BABYLONIA →
(about 500 miles east
of the Jordan River)

Samaria

Jordan River

Mediterranean Sea

•
Bethel

•
Jerusalem

Dead Sea

JUDAH

MOAB

EGYPT

EDOM

SHEBA
(about 1200 miles
southeast of the Dead Sea)

First Kings
Theme: Kingdom Divided

THE BASICS:
⇨ **Who:** **The Author:** The prophet Jeremiah (according to Jewish tradition)

        Main Characters: Solomon, Rehoboam, Elijah, Jezebel

⇨ **What:** A kingdom divided

⇨ **When:** Covers 120 years (971–851 B.C.)

⇨ **Where:** Israel (united); then divided into Israel to the north and Judah to the south

⇨ **Why:** A nation divided against itself cannot stand

MEMORY VERSE: *"For when Solomon was old, his wives turned his heart away after other gods ..."* 1 Kings 11:4

****

REVIEW:

THE PENTATEUCH
⊠ Showed the beginning of the human race (and the Fall) and the chosen race.

⊠ God gave laws for living, so man could be holy as He is holy.

⊠ He gave instructions for building a tabernacle, demonstrating His desire to live among His people.

⊠ God also provided a way for sinful man to approach a Holy God through a blood sacrifice.

THE KINGDOM BOOKS—tell the story of Israel from their conquering the land until their exile.
JOSHUA
⊠ The land was conquered and divided into twelve tribes.

JUDGES
⊠ Because "everyone did what was right in his own eyes," there was immorality, idolatry, and war in the land. However, when the people repented, God rescued them by sending judges to lead them, and then they experienced rest.

RUTH
⊠ A love story of Boaz and Ruth, ancestors of Jesus Christ, which gave a picture of hope through a kinsman-redeemer.

1 SAMUEL
▪ The kingdom was established when the people rejected God as their king and demanded a human king. Saul was the first king.

2 SAMUEL
▪ David, the second king, united the twelve tribes into one great kingdom. In spite of his sin with Bathsheba, David repented, and God called him a man after God's own heart.

First Kings
Theme: Kingdom Divided

OVERVIEW:

- First Kings is the sixth of the seven kingdom books.
- Originally, 1 and 2 Kings were one book.
- According to Jewish tradition, the author of this book was the prophet Jeremiah. However, if it was not him, then it was most certainly one of his contemporaries.
- The main characters include:
  - ~ King Solomon
  - ~ Rehoboam, King Solomon's son
  - ~ Elijah, Israel's prophet
  - ~ King Ahab of Israel
  - ~ Queen Jezebel, Ahab's wicked wife

- After King Saul, David became the king, and he united the twelve tribes into one prosperous kingdom.
- After David's successful reign of forty years, his son Solomon became the king, and it was a glorious time in Israel.
- First Kings covers approximately 120 years from 971 B.C. to 851 B.C.
- The events take place in Israel that was, at first, a united kingdom; however, the kingdom split and became two nations: Israel to the north and Judah to the south.
- First Kings illustrates that a kingdom or a nation that is divided spiritually cannot stand.
- First and 2 Kings show why God sent both kingdoms, Israel and then Judah, into exile.

⇨ **The purpose of 1 Kings is to continue the history of Israel's kings with divided hearts, which resulted in a divided kingdom.**

I. THE KINGDOM WAS UNITED AND THRIVING. (1 KINGS 1–11)

1 Kings 1

- David grew old and sick, and he took to his bed.
- David had become disinterested in ruling the kingdom so his son Adonijah (David's son by Haggith) exalted himself and declared himself king. (1 Kings 1:5–10)
- Nathan went to Bathsheba and encouraged her to remind David that he had sworn that her son, Solomon, would become the next king. (1 Kings 1:11–37)
- Therefore, David anointed Solomon and charged him to walk in obedience to God.

✝ **1 Kings 2:1–4** "As David's time to die drew near, he charged Solomon his son, saying, 'I am going the way of all the earth. Be strong, therefore, and show yourself a man. Keep the charge of the Lord your God, to walk in His ways, to keep His statutes, His commandments, His ordinances, and His testimonies, according to what is written in the Law of Moses, that you may succeed in all that you do and wherever you turn, so that the

Lord may carry out His promise which He spoke concerning me, saying, 'If your sons are careful of their way, to walk before Me in truth with all their heart and with all their soul, you shall not lack a man on the throne of Israel.'"

- Success would only come through walking in God's ways and keeping His commandments.
- The Lord would also carry out His promise that <u>if</u> David's sons walked before God in truth with all their heart and soul, <u>then</u> David would not lack a man on the throne of Israel.
- David also reminded Solomon to deal with Israel's enemies. After David's death, Solomon did so by executing some of them.

A. **King David made a declaration that <u>SOLOMON</u> was to be king and then David died.**

B. **Solomon made his most <u>UNWISE</u> decision just prior to requesting wisdom from God.**

   1. **He made an alliance with <u>EGYPT</u>.**

   2. **He <u>MARRIED</u> one of Pharaoh's daughters.**

> ★ **TEACHING TIP:**
> *What was Solomon thinking? He knew better. His father, David, told him to know and obey ALL the statutes and ALL the laws, including those specifically given by God for kings.*

<u>1 Kings 3</u>
- Solomon, in disobedience to God, not only went to Egypt, but he returned to Israel with an Egyptian as his wife.
  - ~ He had formed a marriage alliance with the daughter of Pharaoh, King of Egypt.
- He brought her to the city of David, and she stayed there until he had finished building his own house and the house of the Lord.

✝ **Deuteronomy 17:16–17** "Moreover, he shall not multiply horses for himself, nor shall he cause the people to return to Egypt to multiply horses, since the Lord has said to you, 'You shall never again return that way.' He shall not multiply wives for himself, or else his heart will turn away; nor shall he greatly increase silver and gold for himself."

First Kings
Theme: Kingdom Divided

> **NOTE:** Kings were not only told what <u>not</u> to do, but also what to do.
> ✝ **Deuteronomy 17:18–20** "Now it shall come about when he sits on the throne of his kingdom, he shall write for himself a copy of this law on a scroll in the presence of the Levitical priests. It shall be with him and he shall read it all the days of his life, that he may learn to fear the Lord his God, by carefully observing all the words of this law and these statutes, that his heart may not be lifted up above his countrymen and that he may not turn aside from the commandment, to the right or the left, so that he and his sons may continue long in his kingdom in the midst of Israel."
> ⇨ **The king was to know AND obey God's Word.**

C. Solomon asked for <u>WISDOM</u> and God gave him wisdom, knowledge, and enormous wealth.

1 Kings 3:6–9

- Solomon prayed and thanked God for His lovingkindness in making him king.
- In his prayer, he also acknowledged that he was young and did not know how to rule so many people.
- Solomon asked God for an understanding heart to judge the people and to discern between good and evil.
- God was very pleased with Solomon's prayer.

✝ **1 Kings 3:10–13** "It was pleasing in the sight of the Lord that Solomon had asked this thing. God said to him, 'Because you have asked this thing and have not asked for yourself long life, nor have asked riches for yourself, nor have you asked for the life of your enemies, but have asked for yourself discernment to understand justice, behold, I have done according to your words. Behold, I have given you a wise and discerning heart, so that there has been no one like you before you, nor shall one like you arise after you. I have also given you what you have not asked, both riches and honor, so that there will not be any among the kings like you all your days.'"

> ★ **TEACHING TIP:**
> *This is a great illustration of how God is able to do far more abundantly beyond all we ask or think! (Ephesians 3:20)*

1 Kings 3:16-28

- Solomon's wisdom was quickly tested when two women came to him with one child. The women had given birth three days apart; however, one of the babies had died. Both claimed that the living child was her own.

- One woman said, "This woman's son died in the night, because she lay on it. So she arose in the middle of the night and took my son from beside me ... and laid her dead son in my bosom."
- The other woman countered, "No! For the living one is my son, and the dead one is your son."
- Solomon displayed the wisdom God had given him with an interesting instruction, "Get me a sword."
  - ~ A sword was brought to him and the king said, "Divide the living child in two, and give half to the one and half to the other."
  - ~ One of the women, the rightful mother, responded, "Oh, my lord, give her the living child, and by no means kill him."
  - ~ The other woman said, "He shall be neither mine nor yours; divide him!"
- King Solomon rendered his decision, "Give the first woman the living child, and by no means kill him. She is his mother."
- The king displayed wisdom in action!

1 Kings 4–5
- King Solomon ruled over all of Israel and he assessed his situation.
- ✝ **1 Kings 5:4–5a** "But now the Lord my God has given me rest on every side; there is neither adversary nor misfortune. Behold, I intend to build a house for the name of the Lord my God, as the Lord spoke to David my father ..."

⇨ **What a God! What a king! What a glorious kingdom! There was peace all around so the people lived in safety and prosperity, and King Solomon acknowledged it all came from God.**

D. The <u>TEMPLE</u> was built and dedicated to the glory of God.

1 Kings 7-8
- Solomon desired to build the temple that had been the dream of his father, David.
- After seven years, it was completed, and he dedicated it.
- Solomon said to the people, "Let your heart therefore be wholly devoted to the Lord our God, to walk in His statutes and to keep His commandments, as at this day." (1 Kings 8:61)
  - ~ He charged them to keep God's commandments—**OBEDIENCE.**
  - ~ He charged them to be wholeheartedly devoted to God—**FAITHFULNESS.**
- This was good advice that Solomon should have followed himself!

First Kings
Theme: Kingdom Divided

E. Solomon's __FAME__ reached through the ancient world.

- God gave Solomon great wisdom and knowledge so that he understood zoology and botany.
- He was also a poet who wrote 3,000 proverbs and 1,005 songs. (1 Kings 4:30–34)
- As Solomon's fame grew, he was inundated with gifts that resulted in his great wealth.

1 Kings 10
- The Queen of Sheba heard about his wisdom and greatness. She came to see for herself.
- ✝ **1 Kings 10:6–10** "Then she said to the king, 'It was a true report which I heard in my own land about your words and your wisdom. Nevertheless I did not believe the reports, until I came and my eyes had seen it. And behold, the half was not told me. You exceed in wisdom and prosperity the report which I heard. How blessed are your men, how blessed are these your servants who stand before you continually and hear your wisdom. Blessed be the Lord your God who delighted in you to set you on the throne of Israel; because the Lord loved Israel forever, therefore He made you king, to do justice and righteousness.' She gave the king a hundred and twenty talents of gold, and a very great amount of spices and precious stones. Never again did such abundance of spices come in as that which the queen of Sheba gave King Solomon."
- And the king's wealth grew.
- Solomon's life seemed to be going well, yet there was a sad aspect to his story.
- Even though he knew God's laws, he did not follow them, especially when it came to his wives.

- ✝ **1 Kings 11:1-2** "Now King Solomon loved many foreign women along with the daughter of Pharaoh: Moabite, Ammonite, Edomite, Sidonian, and Hittite women, from the nations concerning which the Lord had said to the sons of Israel, 'You shall not associate with them, nor shall they associate with you, for they will surely turn your heart away after their gods.' Solomon held fast to these in love."

F. Solomon's many foreign __WIVES__ turned his heart away from God.

- ✝ **1 Kings 11:3-4** "He had seven hundred wives, princesses, and three hundred concubines, and his wives turned his heart away. For when Solomon was old, his wives turned his heart away after other gods; and his heart was not wholly devoted to the Lord his God, as the heart of David his father had been."

G. Solomon's heart was a __DIVIDED__ heart.

- Just as God had warned, Solomon went after the goddess of the Sidonians and the detestable idol of the Ammonites because of his foreign wives.

- He did not follow God fully.
- This disobedience started with a seemingly little sin—"just a trip to Egypt." However, one little sin turned into great disobedience against God.
- Solomon, who once was devoted to God, developed a divided heart.
- Because of his heart condition, the nation would be negatively impacted, and there would be division in the land.

> ❖ **APPLICATION:** There is a principle to be learned and applied from the story of Solomon: ***When you go where you should not go, you bring back what you should not have!***
> ~ We can take our minds or thoughts to places they should not go, so we worry or fantasize.
> ~ We can take our eyes to see things we should not see in books, movies, television, or the internet.
> ~ We can take our mouths where they should not go and gossip, slander, use angry words, or tell lies.
> ~ We can take our feet to the places or people of temptation.
> ~ When we go where we should not go, we are in danger of bringing back things we should not have.

- God had asked for Solomon's heart to be wholly devoted to Him. However, Solomon's heart was divided, and it cost him his descendants and the nation greatly.

✝ **1 Kings 11:9–13** "Now the Lord was angry with Solomon because his heart was turned away from the Lord, the God of Israel, who had appeared to him twice, and had commanded him concerning this thing, that he should not go after other gods; but he did not observe what the Lord had commanded. So the Lord said to Solomon, 'Because you have done this, and you have not kept My covenant and My statutes, which I have commanded you, I will surely tear the kingdom from you, and will give it to your servant. Nevertheless I will not do it in your days for the sake of your father David, but I will tear it out of the hand of your son.'"

- God had appeared twice to Solomon, and yet he still did not obey.

⇨ **Who most represents you: Saul who had no heart for God, David who had a full heart for God, or Solomon who had a divided heart for God?**

II.   THE KINGDOM WAS <u>DIVIDED</u> AND DESTROYED. (1 KINGS 12–22)

- Even with 700 wives and 300 concubines, Solomon apparently had only one son and his name was Rehoboam. (Two daughters are mentioned in 1 Kings 4:11,15.)

First Kings
Theme: Kingdom Divided

- Rehoboam took over as king, but he was not wise like his father.

A. <u>REHOBOAM</u> acted unwisely by disregarding the wisdom of his father, Solomon.

- The people asked Rehoboam to lighten the hard yoke that Solomon had put upon them.

<u>1 Kings 12</u>

- Rehoboam asked for counsel from two groups: the elders and his young peers.
  - ~ The elders advised him to listen to the people, to serve them and grant them their petition by making life easier. Their thought was that such an act would make the people his servants forever.
  - ~ His peers said to tell the people, "Whereas my father loaded you with a heavy yoke, I will add to your yoke; my father disciplined you with whips, but I will discipline you with scorpions' … So the king did not listen to the people." (1 Kings 12:11,15a)

> ★ **TEACHING TIP:**
> *Remember when the people demanded a king? Samuel had warned them that a king would tax them, conscript their children, and put a heavy burden on them.*

⇨ **Rehoboam only inquired of man and not of God. He ignored the godly counsel of the elderly men and instead took the unwise counsel of his friends.**

> ❖ **APPLICATION:** Where do you seek counsel when you need wisdom in making decisions?
> - ~ Is God your first choice?
> - ~ Do you seek the counsel of older, more mature believers?
> - ~ Or do you choose to ask those who will give you an answer that appeals to you, whether it is truthful or not?

B. The once united kingdom was divided into <u>TWO</u> separate nations.

- Because of the harshness of their king, the people revolted and left. The kingdom was divided just as God had said.

1. The <u>NORTHERN</u> ten tribes were called Israel.
  - ~ Jeroboam became the first king over the northern kingdom of Israel.
  - ~ At first, Shechem was the capital.
  - ~ He created idols of golden calves and put them in two places of worship located in Dan and Bethel.

2. The capital was <u>SAMARIA.</u>
- ~ Later, King Omri designated Samaria as the new capital.
- ~ His son, Ahab, built a temple there in which Baal was worshipped.

3. The southern two tribes were called <u>JUDAH.</u>
- ~ Rehoboam reigned over the southern kingdom of Judah.
- ~ Judah was made up of the tribes of Judah and Benjamin.

4. The capital was <u>JERUSALEM.</u>
- ~ The capital continued to be Jerusalem where the temple was located.

⇨ **The once united kingdom had gone from one kingdom to two kingdoms and from serving one God to serving many gods.**

- ▪ Only eight of the twenty kings in Judah were godly. First Kings tells of the reigns of four of Judah's kings:
  1. **Rehoboam** was an evil king.
  2. **Abijam** was also an evil king: "He walked in all the sins of his father which he had committed before him; and his heart was not wholly devoted to the Lord his God, like the heart of his father David." (1 Kings 15:3)
  3. **Asa** was a good king: "Asa did what was right in the sight of the Lord, like David his father ... the heart of Asa was wholly devoted to the Lord all his days." (1 Kings 15:11,14b)
  4. **Jehoshaphat**, the son of Asa, was also a good king: "He walked in all the way of Asa his father; he did not turn aside from it, doing right in the sight of the Lord." (1 Kings 22:43)

<u>1 Kings 15:25–16:34; 22:51–53</u>
- ▪ Not one of the nineteen kings in the northern kingdom of Israel was godly.
- ▪ First Kings covers eight of them, which include: Jeroboam, Nadab, Baasha, Elah, Zimri, Omri, Ahab, and Ahaziah.

⇨ **A divided heart led to a divided kingdom and ungodliness.**

<u>1 Kings 16:19–33</u>
✞ **1 Kings 16:30** "Ahab the son of Omri did evil in the sight of the Lord more than all who were before him.
- ▪ Ahab reigned twenty-two years.
- ▪ He was a king with problems:
  - ~ In disobedience to God's laws for kings, he married Jezebel who was a foreign woman and a pagan worshiper.

~ Together they set up an altar to the goddess Asherah, who was worshipped as the Canaanite "mother of all gods," who was supposedly "life-giving." They also set up the worship of Baal.

C. The once united kingdom was divided into <u>TWO</u> separate nations.

D. <u>ELIJAH</u> was a prophet who God used mightily in warning King Ahab.

<u>1 Kings 17</u>
- Elijah told Ahab that a drought would come into the land because of the idol worship.

<u>1 Kings 18</u>
- Ahab called Elijah a "troubler of Israel." Elijah responded to Ahab's characterization of him
- ✟ **1 Kings 18:18** "I have not troubled Israel, but you and your father's house have, because you have forsaken the commandments of the Lord and you have followed the Baals."

> ✴ **TEACHING TIP:**
> *Jezebel, Ahab's wife, was truly an evil queen because she set about destroying the prophets of the Lord (1 Kings 18:4). Scripture tells us that there were 100 prophets of the Lord hiding in caves under their reign of terror. This is the scene upon which Elijah entered.*

- Elijah challenged Ahab's gods and his 450 prophets of Baal.
- **The Challenge:** The prophets of Baal and Elijah would each prepare a sacrifice without lighting the wood set under it. Then they would call upon their gods, and Elijah would call upon the Lord to light their individual fires. Elijah explained, "Then you call on the name of your god, and I will call on the name of the Lord, and the God who answers by fire, He is God. And the all the people said, 'That is a good idea.'" (1 Kings 18:24)
- **The Purpose of the Challenge:** That the people would know whose god was the true God.
  - ~ The people had divided hearts. Elijah knew that they must make a choice as to whom they would follow.

<u>1 Kings 18:26–29</u>
- The prophets of Baal set up the sacrifice and called upon their god day and night, but there was no answer.
- So they cried louder and cut themselves until blood gushed forth, but there was still no answer.

First Kings
Theme: Kingdom Divided

1 Kings 18:30-39

- Elijah made an altar with stones and dug a trench around it.
- He arranged the wood and a burnt offering, and then he did a very strange thing. He poured water over the wood and offering until the water filled the trench that he had dug! And he prayed.

✜ **1 Kings 18:36b-37** "O Lord, the God of Abraham, Isaac and Israel, today let it be known that You are God in Israel and that I am Your servant and I have done all these things at Your word. Answer me, O Lord, answer me, that this people may know that You, O Lord, are God, and that You have turned their heart back again."

- Then the fire of the Lord fell and consumed the burnt offering, the wood, the stones, and the dust. It licked up the water that was in the trench. God answered Elijah's call to Him!
- When all the people saw this, they fell on their faces; and they said, "The Lord, He is God; the Lord, He is God." (1 Kings 18:39)
- Elijah instructed the people to kill the prophets of Baal.

⇨ **There was a battle between God and Baal, and God won!**

1 Kings 19

- Jezebel hated Elijah because of what he had done to the prophets of Baal.
- She put a death warrant out against him. When Elijah learned of this, he fell into deep despair and did not recall the great things that God had done.
  - ~ He had seen God's power during the drought when God made a widow's bowl of flour and jar of oil multiply at Elijah's request.
  - ~ God had used Elijah to raise a widow's son and defeat the prophets of Baal.

- Elijah ran for his life and said, "... It is enough; now, O Lord, take my life ... I have been very zealous for the Lord, the God of hosts; for the sons of Israel have forsaken Your covenant, torn down Your altars and killed Your prophets with the sword. And I alone am left; and they seek my life, to take it away." (1 Kings 19:4,10)

⇨ **Elijah looked at his fears instead of God's faithfulness.**
  - ~ He had seen miracle after miracle, yet it was as if he now questioned where God was, especially after all Elijah had done for Him. Would God deliver him this time? Had he used up all his miracles?

❖ **APPLICATION:** Elijah is an example of how difficult and unnatural it is to trust God.
  - ~ Have you had moments when you have doubted God and questioned Him: "Will God be there for me this time? Is this one time too many to call for His help?"

First Kings
Theme: Kingdom Divided

⇨ **Fear will bring division in our relationship with God.**

1 Kings 21

- The story of Jezebel continued.
- She did some of the most detestable things in Scripture and is the Bible's prime example of wickedness. *(We do not often name our daughters Jezebel due to its negative connotation.)*
- Though Ahab was the king, it was Jezebel who ruled and controlled Israel.
- The story of King Ahab and Naboth is a good example of Jezebel's control:
  - ~ King Ahab wanted Naboth's vineyard to plant a vegetable garden.
  - ~ Naboth refused, saying, "The Lord forbid me that I should give you the inheritance of my fathers." (1Kings 21:3)
  - ~ Ahab lay down on his bed, turned his face away, and refused to eat. In other words, he had a full-blown "pity party."
  - ~ Jezebel asked her husband why his spirit was so sullen, and he shared how Naboth had refused him his vineyard.
  - ~ Jezebel responded, "Do you now reign over Israel? Arise, eat bread, and let your heart be joyful; I will give you the vineyard of Naboth ..." (1 Kings 21:7)
  - ~ She did get the vineyard for Ahab—by having Naboth murdered!
- Jezebel used her queenly position and influence to do some very evil things.

REVIEW

- ♯ In 1 Samuel, the kingdom was <u>established.</u>
- ♯ In 2 Samuel, the kingdom was <u>united</u> under David.
- ♯ In 1 Kings, the kingdom was <u>divided.</u>
- ♯ When Israel was united, God desired to use her to show other nations how blessed a nation was when they were wholly devoted to God.
- ♯ God wanted other nations to be drawn to Him by what they saw in His people.
- ♯ But when they were disobedient, they were divided, and the glory ended.

⇨ **Disregard of God's Word brought division. That was true in Israel and will also be true in our lives.**

First Kings
Theme: Kingdom Divided

⇨ **PICTURES OF JESUS IN 1 KINGS**

1. Jesus is our WISDOM.

- Though Jesus is concealed throughout the Old Testament, Solomon's wisdom points us to Christ.
- Solomon asked God for wisdom. He was the wisest man who has ever lived.

✝ **1 Kings 3:12** "... Behold, I [God] have given you a wise and discerning heart, so that there has been no one like you before you, nor shall one like you arise after you."

- For us today, Jesus is our wisdom.

✝ **1 Corinthians 1:24** "... but to those who are the called, both Jews and Greeks, Christ the power of God and the wisdom of God."

✝ **1 Corinthians 1:30** "But by His doing you are in Christ Jesus, who became to us wisdom from God ..."

> ❖ **APPLICATION:** Do you need wisdom?
> ~ God tells us, "But if any of you lacks wisdom, let him ask of God, who gives to all generously and without reproach, and it will be given to him." (James 1:5)
> ~ Are you seeking His wisdom?

2. Jesus is All-Powerful and Lord of All.

- Solomon was a wise and powerful king, but Jesus is all-wise and all-powerful, the King of kings.

✝ **Matthew 12:42b** "... and behold, something greater than Solomon is here."

- Jesus is God. Everything in heaven and on earth is His.

FINAL THOUGHTS AND APPLICATION

- ⌑ Disregard of God's Word brought division to His chosen people.
- ⌑ God wants those who are His to be united with Him.
- ⌑ Disregard for God's Word will bring division in our homes, families, workplaces, and nations.
- ⌑ Most of all, disregard of God's Word comes between us and God.

❖ **APPLICATION:** This is a good time for a heart examination. Ask yourself these questions:

1) Do I have an independent spirit?
* ⋆ Do I at times think and act like I know better than God?
* ⋆ Do I at times decide to do things my own way?
* ⋆ Do I seek wisdom apart from God?

→ If we answer "yes" to any of these questions, we are headed for trouble! God wants us to be dependent upon Him.

2) Do I have a fear that remains with me?

→ Someone once said that fear is to Satan what faith is to God.

❖ **FINAL APPLICATION:** Disobedience brings division in our earthly relationships. But mostly it brings division in the fellowship we, as believers, enjoy with God. Disobedience begins when we disregard God's Word; and when disobedience makes its start, the inevitable is a divided heart!

FIRST KINGS REVIEW HELPS ·

✧ **Working together as a team (or divide large group into teams of five or six) put all of the following into chronological order. When the first team is done, stand up! Be ready to tell what each character is most noted for.**

Joshua

Deborah

Abraham

Temple

Aaron

Moses

Noah

David

Samson

Adam

Saul

Joseph

Jonathon

Jacob

Isaac

Pharaoh

Gideon

Samuel

Tabernacle

Serpent (Satan)

Solomon

FIRST KINGS REVIEW HELPS
(Answers for Facilitators)

✧ Working together as a team (or divide large group into teams of five or six) put all of the following into chronological order. When the first team is done, stand up! Here is the order:

Adam

Serpent

Noah

Abraham

Isaac

Jacob

Joseph

Pharaoh (can come before or after Moses)

Moses

Aaron

Tabernacle

Joshua

Deborah

Gideon

Samson

Samuel

Saul

Jonathan (can interchange with David)

David

Solomon

Temple

SECOND KINGS

Kingdoms Exiled

*They rejected His statutes and His covenant which
He made with their fathers and His warnings
with which He warned them.*

2 Kings 17:15

SESSION TWELVE: SECOND KINGS
Kingdoms Exiled

✝ **Memory Verse:** *"They rejected His statutes and His covenant which He made with their fathers and His warnings with which He warned them."* *(2 Kings 17:15)*

- **Introduction: Israel:** 2 Kings covers the reigns of eleven wicked kings of Israel until its captivity by Assyria in 722 B.C. and the reigns of sixteen kings in Judah until it was exiled to Babylon in 586 B.C. Israel and Judah has forsaken their God and, as He had promised, they now suffered the consequences in a foreign land.

- **Oral Review:** Please refer to the **REVIEW Section** in the following Teaching Guide Outline.

- **Homework:** Take time to review and discuss the homework from 1 Kings. Key questions would be:

  Question on Page 155
  Last question on page 159
  All questions on page 162
  All questions on page 165
  Question at the top of page 166

- **Teacher Presentation on the Book of 2 Kings**

- **Learning for Life Discussion questions:** You may choose to discuss all or just one or two of the questions on page 175.

- **Review Helps:** Written review is provided at the end of the teachers' presentation. Because this is the last written review for this set, this part will be done **after** the Teacher Presentation and the discussion.

- **Closing prayer:** Pray for each participant to grow more and more disciplined in the study of God's Word and that, unlike the kings, they would form an even deeper relationship with God and His Son, Jesus Christ.

SECOND KINGS
Theme: Kingdoms Exiled

TIMELINE AID FOR TEACHERS:

⇨ **NOTE: * represents a good king**

ISRAEL

- **2 Kings 1**   King Ahaziah's story is continued from 1 Kings 22:51. He was the son of Ahab.

- **2 Kings 1:17; 3:1**   King Jehoram or Joram, king of Israel. He was the son of Ahab; Ahaziah had no son.

→ *Elijah was taken to heaven in a whirlwind with a chariot of fire. Elisha began to be a prophet to Israel.*

→ *Elisha's miracles: widow's oil, raised dead, multiplied loaves, healed Naaman, axe head floated.*

JUDAH

- **2 Kings 8:16–18**   King Jehoram, king of Judah, son of Jehoshaphat, married Ahab's daughter.

- **2 Kings 8:24–26**   King Ahaziah, son of Jehoram and Athaliah.

ISRAEL

- **2 Kings 9:21–37; 10:11, 25–31**   King Jehu, son of Jehoshaphat, killed Jehoram/Joram(king of Israel), Ahaziah (king of Judah), Jezebel and the house of Ahab, and all Baal worshipers. But Jehu continued worshiping the golden calves and did not walk in the law of the Lord.

JUDAH

- **2 Kings 11:1-16**   Queen Athaliah, mother of King Ahaziah
- **2 Kings 12:1-21**   *Joash or Jehoash, son of Ahaziah

ISRAEL

- **2 Kings 13:1–9**   Jehoahaz, son of Jehu
- **2 Kings 13:10-13**   Jehoash, son of Jehoahaz

JUDAH

- **2 Kings 14:1-22**   *Amaziah, son of Joash

ISRAEL

- **2 Kings 14:23-29**   Jeroboam II, son of Joash/Jehoash

JUDAH

- **2 Kings 15:1-7**   *Azariah/Uzziah, son of Amaziah

SECOND KINGS
Theme: Kingdoms Exiled

ISRAEL
- **2 Kings 15:8–12**   Zechariah, son of Jeroboam II
- **2 Kings 15:13–15**   Shallum, son of Jabesh
- **2 Kings 15:16–22**   Menahem, son of Gadi
- **2 Kings 15:23–26**   Pekahiah, son of Menahem
- **2 Kings 15:27–31**   Pekah, son of Remaliah

JUDAH
- **2 Kings 15:32–38**   *Jotham, son of Azariah/Uzziah
- **2 Kings 16:1-20**   Ahaz, son of Jotham

ISRAEL
- **2 Kings 17:1–41**   Hoshea, son of Elah

JUDAH
- **2 Kings 18:1–20:21**   *Hezekiah, son of Ahaz
- **2 Kings 21:1–18**   Manasseh, son of Hezekiah
- **2 Kings 21:19–26**   Amon, son of Manasseh
- **2 Kings 22:1–23:27**   *Josiah, son of Amon
- **2 Kings 23:28–34**   Jehoahaz, son of Josiah
- **2 Kings 23:34–24:7**   Jehoiakim, son of Josiah
- **2 Kings 24:8–16**   Jehoiachin, son of Jehoiakim
- **2 Kings 24:17-21**   Zedekiah, uncle of the king of Babylon
- **2 Kings 25:22-26**   Gedaliah made governor by the king of Babylon
- **2 Kings 25:27-30**   Jehoiachin released from prison in exile

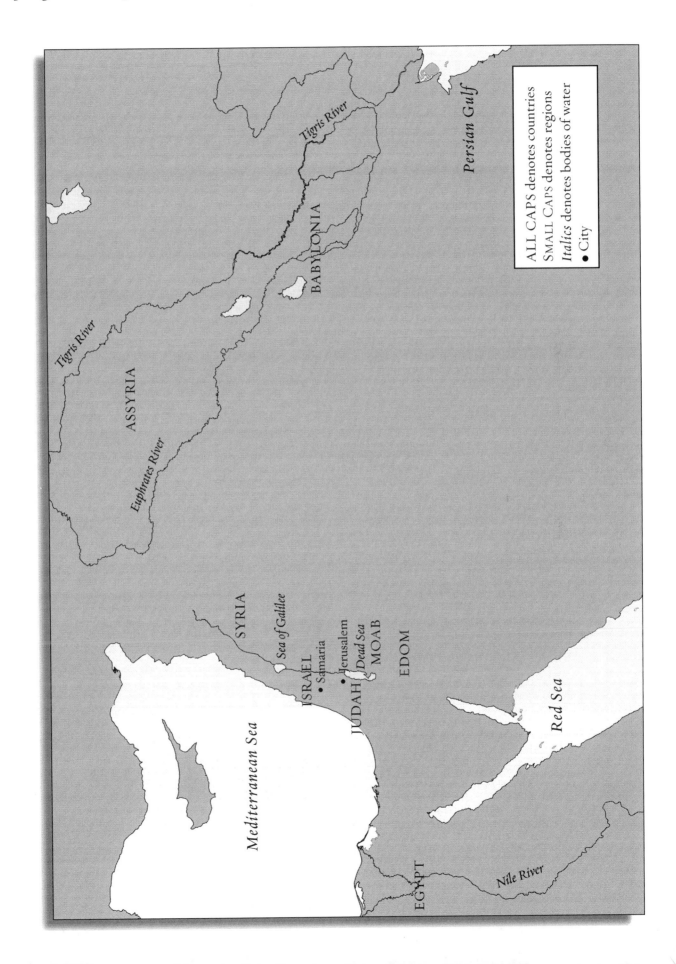

SECOND KINGS
Theme: Kingdoms Exiled

SECOND KINGS
Theme: Kingdoms Exiled

THE BASICS:

⇨ **Who: The Author:** Possibly Jeremiah or the "sons of the prophets"
   Main Characters: Elijah, Elisha, the kings of Israel, the kings of Judah
⇨ **What:** Decline and captivity of the two kingdoms
⇨ **When:** Israel 853–722 B.C., Judah 853–586 B.C., Babylonia 585-560 B.C.
⇨ **Where:** Israel, the northern kingdom, whose capital was Samaria;
   Judah, the southern kingdom, whose capital was Jerusalem;
   Babylonia
⇨ **Why:** The kings led the people away from God, and foreign kings took them into exile

MEMORY VERSE: *"They rejected His statutes and His covenant which He made with their fathers and His warnings with which He warned them." 2 Kings 17:15*

****

REVIEW:

THE PENTATEUCH
⌘ Showed the beginning of the human race (and the Fall) and the chosen race.
⌘ God gave laws for living, so man could be holy as He is holy.
⌘ Abraham's family became a nation. Unbelief kept them from going into the land that God had promised. Instead they wandered for forty years.

JOSHUA
⌘ Joshua led the people to conquer, divide, and settle the land.
⌘ Each of the twelve tribes received a territory.
⌘ Joshua fought enemies in the land and sin in the people. (See Achan in Joshua 7).
⌘ He challenged them to "… choose for yourselves today whom you will serve … but as for me and my house, we will serve the Lord." (Joshua 24:15)
⌘ The people's response to Joshua: "We will serve the Lord our God and we will obey His voice." (Joshua 24:24)

JUDGES
⌘ Judges ruled the land.
⌘ In spite of their good intentions to obey God's voice, many times they did not.
⌘ They were to wipe out all of their enemies, but they did not drive them out completely.
⌘ In misery, they would repent and God would send a judge to rescue and rule over them, and the land would be at rest.
⌘ When the judge died, then everyone would once again do what seemed right in his own eyes and the sin cycle would be repeated.

SECOND KINGS
Theme: Kingdoms Exiled

◻ The nation God chose as the line of the Messiah struggled to follow God with a whole heart.

RUTH

◻ At the same dark time as the Judges, God gave a story of light and hope that involved three people: Naomi, Ruth (Naomi's daughter-in-law), and Boaz.

◻ Naomi and Ruth were in a desperate situation, and Boaz saved them as their kinsman-redeemer. He was related, willing, and able to pay the price to redeem them from their dire circumstances.

1 SAMUEL

◻ The kingdom was established.

◻ God was to be their king, but the people demanded a human king to fight their battles. They wanted to be like other nations.

◻ In spite of Samuel's warnings of dangers and the cost of having a human king, the people persisted.

◻ Their first king, Saul, disobeyed God and "as the leader goes, so go the people."

2 SAMUEL

◻ The kingdom was united. David united the twelve tribes into one prosperous kingdom.

◻ He sinned greatly against Uriah and Bathsheba; however, convicted of sin and broken-hearted over it, he realized his sin was ultimately against God (Psalm 51:4) and he repented. God forgave and restored him.

◻ God called David "a man after God's own heart."

◻ David desired to build a house to God but, because he had shed blood, God said that it would be David's son who would build the temple.

1 KINGS

◻ The kingdom was divided.

◻ When David died, Solomon, his son, became king and the nation was living in peace and prosperity.

◻ Solomon, however, married foreign women who, in his old age, turned his heart away from God, just as God had warned.

◻ Because of this disobedience, God divided the kingdom during the reign of Solomon's son, Rehoboam.

◻ The result was two kingdoms: Israel was made up of ten tribes, and Judah was made up of two tribes (Judah and Benjamin).

◻ Israel in the north had Samaria as its capital and Jeroboam as its king.

◻ Judah in the south had Jerusalem as its capital and Rehoboam as its king.

SECOND KINGS
Theme: Kingdoms Exiled

OVERVIEW:

- Just as 1 and 2 Samuel began as one book, 1 and 2 Kings were also originally one book.
- Sadly, as the book opens, both Israel and Judah were being ruled by men who were less than God's best.
- 2 Kings closes with both kingdoms being taken into exile.

⇨ **God loved His people and did not want them to be exiled or separated from Him or their land.**

Deuteronomy 17:14–17

- God warned the kings:
  - ~ Do not gather for themselves horses which represented prestige and power.
  - ~ Do not gather for themselves money, gold, and silver.
  - ~ Do not intermarry with those from other nations who would introduce idol worship to them.
- But they ignored and violated all of God's laws.

- God was and is so merciful—*__He never gives judgment without first giving warning.__*
- During the time of the kings, God sent many men as prophets.
  - ~ He sent Elijah and Elisha.
  - ~ To the northern kingdom of Israel, He sent Amos and Hosea.
  - ~ To the southern kingdom of Judah, God sent Joel, Isaiah, Micah, Zachariah, Jeremiah, and more because He loved the people and wanted them to love and obey Him.

⇨ **The purpose of 2 Kings is to show the spiritual descent of both Israel and Judah, which led to destruction.**

REVIEW:

- ⌘ In 1 Kings, Elijah was introduced as a prophet in Israel who had victory over the prophets of Baal, King Ahab, and Jezebel.
- ⌘ Elisha was also introduced as the prophet who would follow in the ministry of Elijah, his mentor.
- ⌘ Second Kings begins with Elisha asking for a double portion of Elijah's spirit just before Elijah was taken up by a whirlwind. (2 Kings 2:11)

I. GOD'S WARNINGS WERE GIVEN THROUGH ELIJAH AND <u>ELISHA</u>.

A. After Elijah ascended into heaven, <u>ELISHA</u> succeeded him.

- Second Kings tells of the ministry of Elisha.

SECOND KINGS
Theme: Kingdoms Exiled

- Both Elijah and Elisha were used by God to warn the kings to keep covenant with Him.
- Elisha was mentored by Elijah; yet these two men of the Lord were very different.

ELIJAH	ELISHA
~ Wore the skins or hides of animals around his loins or hips	~ Was from a wealthy family and was known to wear the robes of a teacher
~ Was hairy (or it could be that he wore a garment of hair)	~ Was bald
~ Lived in the wilderness	~ Lived in the city
~ Was a loner—he did not take a disciple until God told him to take Elisha	~ Was known to have at least 100 prophets in training (called "sons of the Prophets"). He discipled them in the truth of God's Word
~ Known to be bold in one minute and cowardly the next	~ Was even-tempered and rarely got angry

2 Kings 1–2
- Elijah was known as the "prophet of fire" (fire and brimstone).
    - In his conflict with the prophets of Baal, he called on God who sent down fire. (1 Kings 18:25–39)
    - He also called on heaven to burn up enemies who were attacking him. (2 Kings 1:9–12)
    - He ascended to heaven escorted by a chariot of fire and horses of fire. (2 Kings 2:11)
- Elisha was a "prophet of water."
    - He purified both contaminated water and stew. (2 Kings 2:19-22)
    - He told Naaman to wash in the Jordan to be healed. (2 Kings 5:1-14)

B. Elisha's ministry to Israel was very **DIFFERENT** from his mentor, Elijah's.

- Not only were the two men very different, but their ministries were different as well.
- Elijah was the forerunner and is compared to John the Baptist, while Elisha points to Jesus Christ.
    - Elijah came first and then Elisha, just as John the Baptist came first and then Jesus.

⇨ **There are parallels, similarities, or pictures of Jesus in Elisha.**

2 Kings 4
- Elisha spoke the truth to the leaders and never ran from confrontation. He knew that "as the leader goes, so go the people."

⇨ **Who else never ran from confrontation and spoke the truth to the people? Jesus! (John 8:1–11)**

SECOND KINGS
Theme: Kingdoms Exiled

- Elisha cared for the suffering. He was the prophet God used to multiply the widow's oil. (2 Kings 4:1–7)

⇨ **Who else had compassion for the suffering? Jesus! (Matthew 9:35–36)**

- Elisha raised a child from the dead. (2 Kings 4:18–37)

⇨ **Who else raised a child from the dead and Lazarus as well? Jesus! (Mark 5:22–24,35–43;   John 11)**

- Elisha multiplied bread and had so much left over that he was able to feed his disciples. (2 Kings 4:42–44)

⇨ **Who else did that? Jesus! (Matthew 15:32-38)**

- Elisha (instructed by God) told Naaman how to be healed from leprosy or death. (2 Kings 5:1–14) No one in those days did anything for lepers, but Elisha showed mercy and helped a leper.

⇨ **Who else reached out, touched, and healed lepers? Jesus! (Mark 1:40-42)**

⇨ **Elisha's ministry demonstrated mercy and compassion, even miracles, while taking care of people. We see pictures of Jesus in his ministry.**

2 Kings 6

- Elisha defied the elements.
  - ~ One of his disciples came to him distraught, sharing that he had lost a borrowed axe in the water. He probably thought it was at the bottom of the river and gone forever.
  - ~ God empowered Elisha to raise the missing axe so that it floated on the water. (2 Kings 6:1–7)

⇨ **Who else defied the elements by changing water into wine, walking on the water, and speaking peace to an angry sea? Jesus! (John 2:7–11; Matthew 8:24–27; Matthew 14:22–28)**

- Elisha performed miracles regarding sight.
  - ~ He opened the eyes of his servant so that he could see chariots of fire or God's army ready to protect him from an enemy army. (2 Kings 6:15-17)
  - ~ He also closed the eyes of the enemy. (2 Kings 6:18)

⇨ **Who else could open eyes and give sight? Jesus! (Luke 18:35–43)**

- Elisha could have called down the chariots of fire to defeat an earthly army, but he did not.

⇨ **Who else could have called down the twelve legions of angels to wipe out the Roman guard in Gethsemane? Jesus! (Matthew 26:51–53)**

C. Elisha's ministry lasted <u>FIFTY</u> years from King Jehoram to King Jehoash.

- The people could see God's power lived out through Elisha who had asked for a double portion of Elijah's spirit.
- God answered that prayer; Elisha showed God's power and His love.

D. God will eventually judge and <u>DISCIPLINE</u> His people.

- Though Elisha was a prophet of love and care, he spoke about judgment in his ministry as well.

<u>**2 Kings 2:23–24**</u>

- He rebuked some young men that "... mocked him and said to him, 'Go up, you baldhead; go up, you baldhead.'"
  - ~ Elisha cursed them in the name of the Lord.
  - ~ Two bears came out of the woods and mauled forty-two of them.

> ★ **TEACHING TIP:**
> *Why would God allow Elisha to do this? He was allowing Elisha to be a just judge. Elisha was representing God, and God will not be mocked.*

<u>**2 Kings 5:20–27**</u>

- Elisha also cursed a servant who was disobedient and was caught in a lie.
- The servant and his descendants had leprosy forever.

⇨ **Jesus is both a loving and compassionate Savior, but He is also our just judge. (John 5:22). And hear this: if God's children continue to ignore His warnings, God will eventually judge and discipline them.**

  - ~ We see this clearly through the words and actions of these prophets.

- Unfortunately, the whole northern kingdom of Israel ignored God's warnings.

II. THE KINGS OF ISRAEL <u>IGNORED</u> GOD'S WARNINGS.

A. All the kings of the northern kingdom were <u>EVIL</u>.

B. The northern kingdom lasted <u>TWO HUNDRED</u> years.

SECOND KINGS
Theme: Kingdoms Exiled

C. Israel had <u>NINETEEN</u> kings.

- All nineteen kings of the northern kingdom were unrighteous.
    - ~ Every one of them lived and ruled apart from God's laws.
    - ~ Of the nineteen, eight were assassinated.
    - * Three were from the evil Omri dynasty.
    - * Five were from the destructive Jehu dynasty.
    - ~ These were truly evil men.
- Ahaziah's story continued from 1 Kings.
- The eleven kings covered in 2 Kings are: Jehoram, Jehu, Jehoahaz, Joash, Jeroboam II, Zechariah, Shallum, Menahem, Pekahiah, Pekah, and Hoshea.

> ★ **TEACHING TIP:**
> *As you read Second Kings, you might want to highlight the name of every king of Israel in blue for these kings made God "blue" or sad. Also highlight the verses that state that all of these kings "did evil in the sight of the Lord and followed in the sins of Jeroboam."*

- The united kingdom lasted approximately 120 years.
- Israel continued approximately 209 years longer.
- Judah (the southern kingdom) remained a nation alone for another 136 years.
- Every one of their reigns was marked with unrest, bloodshed, war, evil, and idolatry.
- These were sad and unrestful times for God's people.

D. God <u>REMOVED</u> Israel from His sight.

E. In 722 B.C., the Assyrians conquered Israel and <u>SCATTERED</u> the ten tribes.

✞ **2 Kings 17:18a** "So the Lord was very angry with Israel and removed them from His sight" ...
- ~ How sad! God allowed the Assyrians to come in and kill, capture, and conquer Israel; and He allowed some of His surviving people to be exiled.

<u>2 Kings 17:23–33</u>
- Many foreigners were brought in to repopulate the land.
    - ~ These foreigners intermarried with the remaining Israelites, which resulted in Samaritans, a people who were mixed nationalities and religions.
- All ten tribes were killed or scattered.

> **NOTE:** The Assyrians were ruthless and cruel conquerors. They were known for doing three things to their captives in order to fully intimidate them into submission:
> 1. They would impale the leaders of a conquered city. Impaling means that they would drive a stake through the leader's body then stand him upright leaving him to slowly die.
> 2. They would go through the city they had just destroyed and mutilate the bodies of the dead by decapitating them. They would take the heads and pile them up outside the city as a "monument" to their own cruelty.
> 3. The captives who survived were not any more fortunate than those who died. They were taken away, not just in chains, but with hooks through their faces or lips!

- This was death, destruction, and devastation.

⇨ **These evil kings who led their people into worshipping Baal and the golden calves also led God's chosen people straight into devastation and destruction.**

⇨ **When you are exiled from God, you are in captivity to something, and it is always cruel.**

III. THE KINGS OF <u>JUDAH</u> IGNORED GOD'S WARNINGS.

A. Judah had <u>TWENTY</u> kings.

B. Only <u>EIGHT</u> kings did what was right.

C. God removed <u>JUDAH</u> from His presence.

- The southern kingdom of Judah with its capital in Jerusalem did not do much better than the northern kingdom.
- Judah was made up of only two tribes: Judah and Benjamin.
- The eight good kings were:
  - ~ Asa (1 Kings)   ~ Azariah
  - ~ Jehoshaphat   ~ Jotham
  - ~ Joash   ~ Hezekiah
  - ~ Amaziah   ~ Josiah

> ★ **TEACHING TIP:**
> *You might want to highlight Judah's kings in yellow because Judah was the line preserved by God to be the line of the Messiah. Also highlight the phrase "The king did right in the sight of the Lord according to all their father David had done."*

SECOND KINGS
Theme: Kingdoms Exiled

__2 Kings 12:3; 14:3-4; 15:4__ (Note: there are other scriptures but this is a good sampling)

- Though good kings, all of them, except Josiah, tragically allowed the high places for idol worship and sacrifice to remain.

2 Kings 24:20

~ These kings allowed idolatry to continue, and "as the leader goes, so go the people."

~ The anger of the Lord came on Jerusalem and Judah until He cast them from His presence.

D. The __BABYLONIANS__ conquered the southern tribes in 586 B.C.

E. The people were taken to Babylon in __EXILE__ for seventy years.

2 Kings 24-25

- It was 136 years after the fall of the northern kingdom of Israel when God allowed the Babylonians to come in and exile the southern kingdom of Judah.
- There were three deportations:
  1) In 605 B.C., Nebuchadnezzar took captive the brightest, which included Daniel and his three friends.
  2) In 597 B.C., Nebuchadnezzar returned and took King Jehoiachin and Ezekiel captive along with 10,000 leading citizens, which included all craftsmen and the smiths.
  3) In 586 B.C., Nebuchadnezzar came with the final destruction of Jerusalem.
     * Though a remnant of Judah would return, the people were exiled from the land for seventy years.

⇨ **There are lessons to be learned from several of the kings.**

1) Joash (or Jehoash) - 2 Kings 11:2; 12:2–18; 2 Chronicles 24

- He was a child king.
- Queen Athaliah, the daughter of evil King Ahab and Queen Jezebel, ordered that all the royal offspring be destroyed after her son King Ahaziah of Judah died.
- This act of destruction would have ended the line of King David; but God used a relative to save the baby, Joash, who was in the line of David. A good reminder that God always keeps His promises.
- During Queen Athaliah's six-year reign, she broke into the house of God and used the holy things of the Lord for Baal worship!
- When Joash was seven years old (835 B.C.), he was crowned the king of Judah.
- He did right in the sight of the Lord and repaired the damaged temple. (2 Kings 12:2–18, 2 Chronicles 24:1–19).

- Later, however, he allowed the officials of Judah to serve the Asherim and the idols. The priest Zechariah confronted Joash: "Why do you transgress the commandments of the Lord ...? Because you have forsaken the Lord, He has also forsaken you." (2 Chronicles 24:20)
- Instead of listening to Zechariah, Joash had him killed!
- Later, the servants of Joash conspired against him and had him assassinated in his own bed. (2 Chronicles 24:25)

⇨ **After starting well, Joash ended poorly.**

2) Josiah - 2 Kings 22; 2 Chronicles 35:20–24

- He was also a child king; he was eight years old when he began to reign.
- At approximately age twenty-six, a copy of God's Word was brought to him. When he heard the words of the Book of the Law, he tore his clothes and told the priests:

✝ **2 Kings 22:13** "Go, inquire of the Lord for me and the people and all Judah concerning the words of this book that has been found, for great is the wrath of the Lord that burns against us, because our fathers have not listened to the words of this book, to do according to all that is written concerning us."

- God told the people:

✝ **2 Kings 22:17** "Because they have forsaken Me and have burned incense to other gods that they might provoke Me to anger with all the work of their hands, therefore My wrath burns against this place, and it shall not be quenched."'

- To Josiah, God said:

✝ **2 Kings 22:19–20** "'... because your heart was tender and you humbled yourself before the Lord when you heard what I spoke against this place and against its inhabitants that they should become a desolation and a curse, and you have torn your clothes and wept before Me, I truly have heard you,' declares the Lord. 'Therefore, behold, I will gather you to your fathers, and you will be gathered to your grave in peace, and your eyes will not see all the evil which I will bring on this place ...'"

- Josiah brought about revival by putting away idols, removing mediums, and reinstituting Passover.
- However, it did not end well for Josiah.
  - ~ Though warned not to fight with Pharaoh Neco, Josiah went to war against Neco and was shot by the archers and died.

SECOND KINGS
Theme: Kingdoms Exiled

3) Hezekiah - 2 Kings 18–20

- He began to reign in 715 B.C. at the age of twenty-five.
- He started as a strong leader.

✝ **2 Kings 18:3–4** "He did right in the sight of the Lord, according to all that his father David had done. He removed the high places and broke down the sacred pillars and cut down the Asherah. He also broke in pieces the bronze serpent that Moses had made, for until those days the sons of Israel burned incense to it …"

> ★ **TEACHING TIP:**
> *This verse also shows that man is religious by nature. We can turn even good, God-given things, such as the bronze serpent of Moses, into idols.*

- Hezekiah was not like the people:

✝ **2 Kings 18:6–7** "For he clung to the Lord; he did not depart from following Him, but kept His commandments, which the Lord had commanded Moses. And the Lord was with him; wherever he went he prospered. And he rebelled against the king of Assyria and did not serve him."

- God even had Hezekiah commission his scribes to compile part of the book of Proverbs. (Proverbs 25:1)

- Tragically, Hezekiah made a deal with the king of Assyria. This involved Hezekiah giving the king of Assyria all the silver in the house of the Lord. He also cut off the gold from the doors of the temple to give to this king. (2 King 18:14–16)

- The Assyrians taunted Hezekiah, telling him not to listen to the Lord. God sent the prophet Isaiah to encourage him.

✝ **2 Kings 19:6–7** "Isaiah said to them, 'Thus you shall say to your master, 'Thus says the Lord, 'Do not be afraid because of the words that you have heard, with which the servants of the king of Assyria have blasphemed Me. Behold, I will put a spirit in him [the Assyrian king] so that he will hear a rumor and return to his own land. And I will make him fall by the sword in his own land.'''

- Hezekiah received a threatening letter from the Assyrians.

✝ **2 Kings 19:11** "Behold, you have heard what the kings of Assyria have done to all the lands, destroying them completely. So will you be spared?"

- ~ In fear, Hezekiah took the letter before the Lord. He first praised God for being the God of Israel and the Creator of all the earth and all the kingdoms on it. He then asked God to hear his prayer and save them. (2 Kings 19:14–20)

- ~ God heard his prayer and that night the angel of the Lord went out and struck dead 185,000 men in the camp of the Assyrians. And Sennacherib, the king of Assyria, returned home just as God had said. (2 Kings 19:35–36)

- Hezekiah became mortally ill. Isaiah spoke to him, "Thus says the Lord, 'Set your house in order, for you shall die and not live.'" (2 Kings 20:1b)

- When Hezekiah heard this:

✟ **2 Kings 20:2–3** "… he turned his face to the wall and prayed to the Lord, saying, 'Remember now, O Lord, I beseech You, how I have walked before You in truth and with a whole heart and have done what is good in Your sight.' And Hezekiah wept bitterly."

- And God responded to Hezekiah:

✟ **2 Kings 20:5b–6** "I have heard your prayer, I have seen your tears; behold, I will heal you. On the third day you shall go up to the house of the Lord. I will add fifteen years to your life, and I will deliver you and this city from the hand of the king of Assyria; and I will defend this city for My own sake and for My servant David's sake."

- Once again, a good start had a tragic end, for in those fifteen additional years, Hezekiah's pride got the best of him.
  - When the Babylonians came, he showed off all the treasures in his kingdom to them. Isaiah informed Hezekiah that all of the treasures he had paraded before the Babylonians (treasures he and his fathers had stored up for themselves) would be carried off to Babylon. Nothing would be left, and this is exactly what happened.
  - Even more tragic, during this gift of fifteen additional years, Hezekiah had a son, Manasseh, who would become the most evil king Judah would ever have!

4) Manasseh - 2 Kings 21; 2 Chronicles 33:1–20

- He became king when he was twelve years old (697 B.C.) and reigned for fifty-five years.

- To say that the reign of King Manasseh started poorly would be an understatement.
  - He built altars to Baal.
  - He set idols in the house of the Lord.
  - He worshiped and served all the host of heaven.
  - He was into witchcraft, sorcery, divination, and mediums.
  - He even made his children pass through fire, sacrificing them to other gods!

- God's responded to his reign:

✟ **2 Kings 21: 11–13** "Because Manasseh king of Judah has done these abominations, having done wickedly more than all the Amorites did who were before him, and has also made Judah sin with his idols; therefore thus says the Lord, the God of Israel, 'Behold, I am bringing such calamity on Jerusalem and Judah, that whoever hears of it, both his ears will tingle. I will stretch over Jerusalem the line of Samaria and the plummet of the house of Ahab, and I will wipe Jerusalem as one wipes a dish, wiping it and turning it upside down.'"

SECOND KINGS
Theme: Kingdoms Exiled

- ▪ God used the Assyrians to "wipe Jerusalem."
  - ~ They captured Manasseh, bound him in chains with hooks in his face, and took him to Babylon.
- ¤ It was in his captivity that Manasseh realized just how far he was from God. He called out to God and repented.
  - ~ God heard him and restored him, taking him back to Judah.
  - ~ Manasseh removed the foreign gods and idols he had built there.

⇨ **Manasseh started poorly but ended well.**

⇨ **IMPORTANT TO NOTE: After the exile, there would never again be idol worship in Israel.**

⇨ ## PICTURES OF JESUS IN 2 KINGS
  - ~ Referenced earlier on pp 5–6

FINAL THOUGHTS AND APPLICATION

- ¤ Second Kings shows that God's plans and His promises cannot be thwarted.
  - ~ Although Queen Athaliah attempted to destroy the line of David, God protected that line by saving Joash, and Jesus came as a direct descendant.
  - ~ God kept His promise to David to have a descendant from his line on the throne forever.

- ¤ There are lessons that we can learn and apply from the kings in this book:
  - **a) It is not how we start our walk with the Lord, but how we finish it!**
    - ⋆ The life of Joash illustrates a life that started well, but ended poorly due to complacency, pride, and not listening to God.
    - ⋆ Make it your goal and prayer to finish strong!

  - **b) It is vital that we spend time in God's Word.**
    - ⋆ Josiah's life reveals the power of the Word of God to bring conviction that leads to repentance, which can change the course of a family or nation.
    - ⋆ Are you like Josiah with a heart that is tender to the Word of God? Do you humble yourself and obey what God says?

c) Our prayer life should be centered on God's will for our lives, not our own self-conceived plans.

* Hezekiah prayed a self-centered prayer when he demanded a longer life. He did not use that time for the glory of God, instead it produced Judah's most evil king.
* Be careful what you pray for, you might get it! (Examine your motives!)

d) God can restore the disobedient and use them for His glory when authentic repentance occurs.

* Manasseh's story is a testimony that encourages us because it clearly illustrates that, even if we start poorly, we can finish well.
* If God did this for Manasseh (the most evil king in Judah), then He can do it for you. It is an encouragement to know that no one is a "lost cause" when God is involved!

❖ **APPLICATION:** God's people are to listen to His Word, obey His commands, and heed His warnings so that we are not exiled from His presence.

❖ **FINAL APPLICATION:** As the leader goes, so go the people? Who are you leading? Where are you taking them?

SECOND KINGS REVIEW HELPS
(Review of the Kingdom Books)

1. How many books are in the Kingdom books?

2. What are the names of the books in the Pentateuch?

3. Which Kingdom book tells of the life of King David?

4. Which Pentateuch book includes the last three sermons of Moses?

5. What are the names of the seven Kingdom books?

6. Who succeeded Moses in leadership?

7. Who was given three promises by God?
   * What were those three promises?

8. What king built the temple?

9. Where was the temple?
   * In what book was this done?

10. What was the tabernacle?
    * In what book was it built?

11. Under what king was the kingdom divided?

12. What was the name of the two kingdoms after they were divided?

13. Who was the last judge of Israel?

14. Who was the first king of Israel?

15. What king was a "man after God's own heart"?

16. In what book did the people conquer the Promised Land?

17. What country exiled Judah? Where did they take them?

18. What nation conquered Israel?

19. What kingdom was conquered first? Why?

Second Kings Review Helps
(Answers for Facilitators)

1. How many books are in the Kingdom books? **Seven**

2. What are the names of the books in the Pentateuch? **Genesis, Exodus, Leviticus, Numbers, Deuteronomy**

3. Which Kingdom book tells of the life of King David? **2 Samuel**

4. Which Pentateuch book includes the last three sermons of Moses? **Deuteronomy**

5. What are the names of the seven Kingdom books? **Joshua, Judges, Ruth, 1 Samuel, 2 Samuel, 1 Kings, 2 Kings**

6. Who succeeded Moses in leadership? **Joshua**

7. Who was given three promises by God? **Abraham**
   * What were those three promises? **People, Land, Blessing**

8. What king built the temple? **Solomon**

9. Where was the temple? **Jerusalem**
   * In what book was it built? **1 Kings**

10. What was the tabernacle? **A tent for worship**
    * In what book was it built? **Exodus**

11. Under what king was the kingdom divided? **Rehoboam**

12. What was the name of the two kingdoms after they were divided? **Israel, Judah**

13. Who was the last judge of Israel? **Samuel**

14. Who was the first king of Israel? **Saul**

15. What king was a "man after God's own heart"? **David**

16. In what book did the people conquer the Promised Land? **Joshua**

17. What country exiled Judah? **Babylon**
    * Where did they take them? **Babylon**

18. What nation conquered Israel? **Assyria**

19. What kingdom was conquered first? **Israel**
    * Why? **Did not have the temple, King was not a descendant of David, no priests from line of Aaron**

THE KINGDOM

BOOKS

AT A GLANCE

****

CHARTS

SET 2

THE KINGDOM BOOKS AT A GLANCE

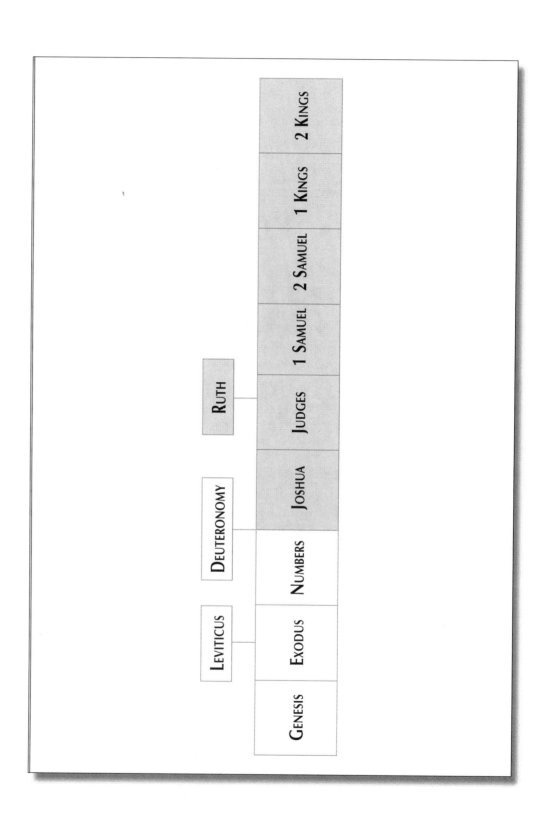

Joshua

CONQUEST		SETTLEMENT	
Entering the Land	Conquering the Land	Partitioning the Land	Living in the Land
1　　　　5	6　　　　12	13　　　21	22　　　24

Joshua

Who Displayed Faith	How They Displayed Faith	Result of Their Faith

JUDGES

Causes of Failure	Cycles of Failure	Consequences of Failure
1:1 3:4	3:5 16:31	17:1 21:25

JUDGES

The Cycles	1st Cycle 3:7-11	2nd Cycle 3:12-30	3rd Cycle 4:1–5:31	4th Cycle 6:1–8:32
People Rebelled				6:1
God Rejected				Midian 7 years 6:1
People Repented				6:6-7
God Sent Rescuer (Judge)				Gideon 6:11–8:28
Period of Rest				40 years 8:28

JUDGES

JOSHUA	JUDGES
Obedience	Disobedience
Belief	Unbelief
Progress	Decline
Unity	Disunity
Joy	Sorrow
Faithfulness	Faithlessness
Victory	Defeat

JUDGES

Ruth

RUTH	ESTHER
A Gentile who married a Jew	A Jew who married a Gentile
Book begins with a famine	Book begins with a feast
Book ends with the birth of a baby	Book ends with the death of 75,000 people
She became an ancestress of the Messiah	She became a savior of the Messiah's people
God is mentioned 25 times	God is not mentioned once

Ruth

Ruth's Commitment to Naomi	Ruth's Introduction to Boaz	Ruth's Request of Boaz	Ruth's Marriage to Boaz
Chapter 1	Chapter 2	Chapter 3	Chapter 4

Ruth

	Boaz	**Jesus**
He had to be a near kinsman.	Ruth 2:1,3,20; 3:12-13	John 1:14 Philippians 2:5-8 Hebrews 2:17
He had to be willing to redeem.	Ruth 2:8; 3:11	Mark 10:45 Luke 19:10
He had to have the price of redemption.	Ruth 2:1; 4:9-10	1 Peter 1:18-19 Hebrews 9:11-14

RUTH

JUDGES	RUTH
Disloyalty	Loyalty
Unfaithfulness	Faithfulness
Hate	Love
Disobedience	Obedience
Lust	Purity
Cruelty	Kindness
War	Peace
Battlefield	Harvest Field
Dark Sky	Bright Star

I SAMUEL

Samuel: The Last Judge	Saul: The First King	Saul & David: The First King and King Elect
1 8	9 15	16 31

2 SAMUEL

Triumphs of David	Transgressions of David	Troubles of David	Testimony of David
1 10	11 12	13 21	22 24

2 Samuel

Promise	Fulfillment
1. "I will make you a great name" (7:9).	2 Samuel 8:13-14
2. "I will also appoint a place for My people Israel" (7:10).	2 Samuel 8:3 (referring to the Euphrates River)
3. "I will give you rest from all your enemies" (7:11).	1 Kings 5:1-4; 1 Chronicles 22:6-9

1 KINGS

David's Last Days	Solomon's Reign	Division of the Kingdom	Elijah's Ministry
1 2	3 11	12 16	17 22
United Kingdom		Divided Kingdom	
One Nation Becomes Two			

2 KINGS

Continued Decline of Israel and Judah	Capivity of Israel by Assyria	Continued Decline of Judah	Capivity of Judah by Babylonia
1 12	13 17	18 23	24 25
Divided Kingdom		Surviving Kingdom	
Two Nations Become None			

2 Kings

1 Kings	2 Kings
Opens with David, king of Israel	Closes with Nebuchadnezzar, king of Babylonia
Solomon's glory	Jehoiachin's shame
The temple built and consecrated	The temple violated and destroyed
Begins with blessings for obedience	Ends with judgment for disobedience
The growth of apostasy	The consequences of apostasy
The united kingdom is divided	The two kingdoms are destroyed

2 Kings

605 BC	597 BC	586 BC
King Jehoiakim	King Jehoiachin	King Zedekiah
2 Kings 24:1-7	2 Kings 24:8-16	2 Kings 24:17–25:21

OLD TESTAMENT BOOKS

CHRONOLOGICAL RELATIONSHIP OF THE OLD TESTAMENT BOOKS

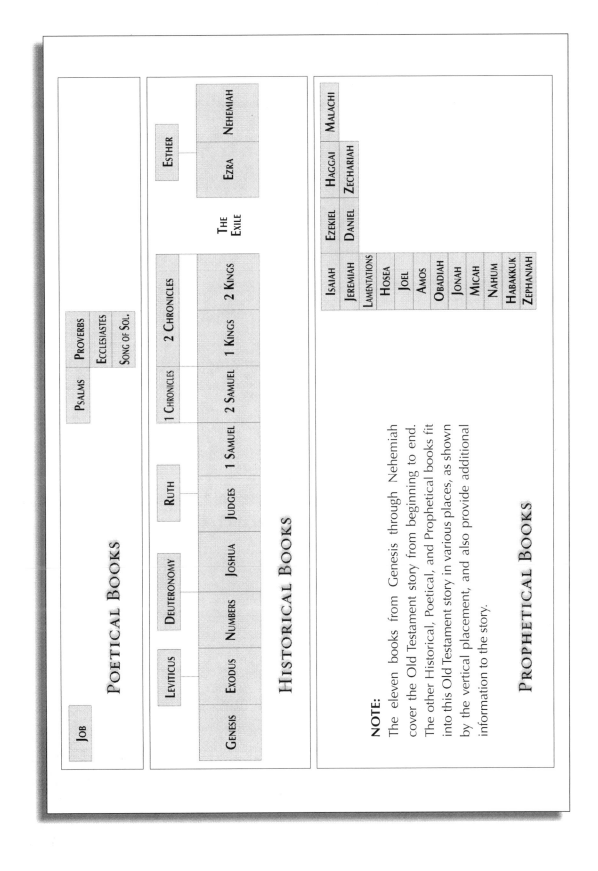

NOTE:
The eleven books from Genesis through Nehemiah cover the Old Testament story from beginning to end. The other Historical, Poetical, and Prophetical books fit into this Old Testament story in various places, as shown by the vertical placement, and also provide additional information to the story.

POETICAL BOOKS

				PSALMS	PROVERBS
					ECCLESIASTES
					SONG OF SOL.

JOB

HISTORICAL BOOKS

					1 CHRONICLES	2 CHRONICLES
GENESIS	EXODUS	NUMBERS	JOSHUA	JUDGES	1 SAMUEL	2 SAMUEL	1 KINGS	2 KINGS

LEVITICUS · DEUTERONOMY · RUTH

ESTHER

EZRA · NEHEMIAH

THE EXILE

PROPHETICAL BOOKS

ISAIAH	EZEKIEL	HAGGAI	MALACHI
JEREMIAH	DANIEL	ZECHARIAH	
LAMENTATIONS			
HOSEA			
JOEL			
AMOS			
OBADIAH			
JONAH			
MICAH			
NAHUM			
HABAKKUK			
ZEPHANIAH			

Made in the USA
Columbia, SC
13 August 2024